The Enigmatic Life And Work Of Agatha Christie

GEW Humanities Group

Global East-West. London

Copyright © 2025 by GEW Humanities Group

"What Do You Know About?"   A Global East-West Series

Edited by Hichem Karoui.

All rights reserved. No part of this book may be reproduced in any manner whatsoever without written permission, except for brief quotations incorporated into critical articles and reviews.

First printing, 2025.

Contents

1. Introduction to Agatha Christie's Literary Dominion — 1

2. Formative Years
   Torquay to the First Tale — 17

3. The Birth of a Genre
   Early Works and Breakthroughs — 31

4. Unraveling Intricacies
   Deception and Human Psychology in Her Work — 47

5. Poirot, Marple, and Iconic Characters
   Building Legends — 65

6. The War's Influence
   Nursing, Pharmacy, and Tragedy — 81

7. Exotic Inspirations   97
    Travels with Max Mallowan

8. From Page to Screen   113
    Adapting Agatha for New Audiences

9. The Vanishing Act   131
    Christie's Own Life Mystery

10. A Lasting Impact   147
    The Legacy of the Queen of Crime

Selected Bibliography   163

1

Introduction to Agatha Christie's Literary Dominion

Introduction to Agatha Christie's Literary Dominion

Agatha Christie's influence on the world of detective fiction is unparalleled, as she essentially laid its foundational principles. Even today, her innovation and mastery of deeply intricate plotlines continue to captivate readers, serving as a testament to the timeless appeal of her work. Through evocative and imaginative storytelling, Christie was the first to incorporate deep mystery and intrigue into fiction, allowing readers to enjoy the challenging mental stimulation provided through the enigmatic puzzles she crafted. Christie's undeniable understanding of human nature and tenacious drive for realism give her stories the resonance required to connect with audiences of different ages and time periods. Christie's mastery of weaving sophisticated societal commentary and acute observation with elaborate puzzles serves to further strengthen her position as a literary icon. It is clear that Christie's work has endured the sands of time, emerging as distinctive signposts for both seasoned authors and neophytes, and her works, richly diverse in culture, have fostered unmatched global influence. An exploration of Christie's vast fictional universe reveals how much her influence spans beyond mere detective fiction.

Agatha Christie's work transcends the boundaries of detective fiction, making significant contributions to the fields of psychology, sociology, and storytelling. Her complex narratives profoundly understand human behaviour, morality, and the eternal quest for truth. By delving into her themes, readers not only find relief from the mundane but also gain insights that prompt deep reflections on humanity. In the following chapters, we will embark on a fascinating journey into the world of Agatha Christie, exploring the intricate nuances of her art and the enduring masterpiece that continues to inspire lovers of refined literature.

The Enigma of Her Unique Storytelling

Agatha Christie's storytelling has captivated readers for generations, and her ability to weave intricate plots with subtle clues and breathtaking denouements remains unmatched within the world of mystery literature. Blending intellect and intuition and meticulous planning while crafting an organic story keep the readers engaged until the very last revelation. Christie's narratives are not only about solving a crime but also lead the reader to delve deep into the human psyche, reflect societal nuances, and marvel at the creation of blended intrigue. The puzzles she has constructed are bound to stir curiosity within her audience. Christie's storytelling rests on her unique understanding of human nature, crafting deeply resonating characters and situations. Masterfully orchestrating the rise and fall of suspense within the novel, she creates tension that keeps her audience captivated till the last page. Texts are brought to life under her distinct narrative charm where the mundane meets the extraordinary, life processes turned into art, and the world moulded into wonder.

Christie's stories, with their captivating settings, intriguing secrets, and multidimensional characters, can be rightly called intricate masterpieces. With each story, she ensnares her readers in a mysterious web, leaving them eagerly anticipating the resolution. Her prose, with its breathtaking elegance and sophistication, creates a spellbinding atmosphere that immerses the audience and motivates them to uncover the marked secrets within her mystical pages. Her impact on contemporary literature is evident in the works of authors who strive to blend emotion with intellectual rigour, inspired by Christie's remarkable storytelling. Her enduring skill in captivating storytelling through rich, veiled mystery ensures her timeless literary significance. Her as-of-yet unsolved literary riddles grant her the recognition as a master storyteller, shaping the imaginations of innumerable readers.

Craftsmanship: The Art of Suspense and Surprise

Christie's craftsmanship is apparent in her skilful suspense-building, plotting, and weaving together intriguing overt narratives and unexpected plot twists. Special elements in her stories contribute to her mastery of suspense. Tension and anticipation are built due to every gesture having hidden meaning and every clue being placed precisely, greatly contributing to the overarching piece. As the story progresses through carefully ordered piece-by-piece revelation of critical information, her readers are left on the edge, waiting to uncover the solution to Christie's complex riddles. Misdirection and red herrings employed also showcase Christie's skilful mastery. The overwhelming sensation of disarray is expertly intertwined with the sparkling clarity at the story's climax. Her interweaving of multiple subplots enhances her storyteller skill and guarantees an unparalleled reading journey. In addition, rich and deeply nuanced characters, crafted through Christie's knowledge of human nature, undoubtedly enable profound drama to unfold.

Christie deepens the tension further by fusing her characters' lives, motives, and secrets into the central mysteries, turning the solution into a deep understanding rather than just a logical conclusion. This adds a layer of complexity that reveals the depths of sociological constructs. The world of literature has wisely benefited from Christie's ingenious storytelling because she has always been, and still remains, a standard bearer of fiction who has inspired countless writers and continues to amaze people globally. Her storytelling has not only entertained but also inspired and enriched the literary landscape, leaving readers and writers alike in awe of her skill and creativity.

Characterisation: Breathing Life into Fiction

A remarkable attribute of Christie's work is her ability to create intriguing characters tailored to specific contexts, which is what makes her stand out as a writer. Coming to life in the rich world of Agatha Christie, these characters are thoughtfully crafted by her keen insight into psychology combined with her imagination, ensuring that they will be remembered many decades into the future. Each character is described fully as a living being possessing multifaceted traits that bring them to life, making certain they are unforgettable to the readers long after they finish reading the book. This depth of character draws readers into the narrative, creating an emotional investment in the story.

From the sophisticated Hercule Poirot to the shrewd Miss Marple, Christie's protagonists are more than just detectives – they are rich in cultural depth and possess distinct traits and moral frameworks. Each of them contains an essence, which reflects onto the landscape of humanity, revealing the multitude of ways people think and feel. In addition, Christie's secondary characters and antagonists are painted with vivid strokes, illustrating how everyone within her fictive worlds is nurtured in imagination by her skilful pen.

In addition, Christie's figures are connected to the entwined intricacies of the story, whose actions and responses catalyse movement in the plot. Every character contributed to the mystery in some form, from the suspects' interlaced motives to the hidden agendas behind harmless façades. This complementarity concerning character and plot demonstrates Christie's ability to give readers sophisticated yet captivating narratives.

Beyond her iconic detectives and all the antagonists, Christie's skill of transforming even the most niche characters into people with rich backstories and nuances is astonishing. Every character, irrespective of the length of their portrayal, has a unique persona, background, and prominence that plays a part in building the intricate whole of the story. This meticulousness brings incomparable wealth to her works as each character plays an important part in the story while connecting with the readers on a profoundly personal level.

To conclude, Agatha Christie's works of unfaltering mastery and ingenuity in characterisation transform her stories beyond just puzzles and thrillers into timeless pieces that reflect the deepest layers of humanity. It is an imprint that ensures her characters will always stand in history as a testament to her vivid imagination and fiction-filled world, forever marking the literary world as apostrophic, realising their fiction, and truly making her the unmatched Queen of Crime.

The Impact of Time and Society on Her Stories

Agatha Christie's stories are masterpieces that tell us about the society and culture of her timelines. The rough period of the early 20th century shaped Christie's backstory because it faced two world wars, economic downturns, and strong societal shifts. Additionally, having wars during that time supported the emergence of new themes like uncertainty and industrialisation in her stories. Christie's observation of human behaviour, alongside dictating the spirit of the time in her output, was evident in nearly all of her works. Narratives from the post-war periods showcased society's distrust and uncertainty in healing itself after wars. Furthermore, the social changes showcased in women's societal roles, like Miss Marple and Tuppence Beresford, demonstrate gender and social dynamics between the interwar and post-war eras. Each tale had unique themes due to the rich tapestry of worldwide social and cultural changes during the decades, which were splendid for Christie to infuse in her mysteries.

Furthermore, her narratives were enriched by the impact of colonialism, global travel, and the emergence of new geopolitical powers. Christie showcased her mastery in intertwining world pulse with international affairs, from the splendour of the Egyptian archaeological digs to the mesmerising Orient Express and the espionage whispers of the Cold War. She effortlessly captured readers' interests with the charm of foreign lands and the political espionage mystery. Additionally, the moral and sociological societal changes from the mid-20th century are based on Christie's exploration of the themes of justice, conscience, and truth and the integral nature of these concepts in her stories. Amidst the post-war fury, a quest for vengeance battling with voluminous crime evoked confrontation with morality. Christie's dissection of human ethics was poignant and turbulent as society transformed rapidly. Strikingly, her infusion of logic alongside emotion renders these themes strong, casting Christie as one of the pioneers in detective fiction literature and a chronicler of these eras.

Christie's life and works reveal the intricate influences that shaped her literary creations. In other words, Agatha Christie's stories demonstrate the relationship between history and literature and provide an alluring glimpse into the many aspects that influenced her enduring stories.

Recurring Themes: Justice, Morality, and Intrigue

Agatha Christie's literary legacy is marvelled at for her mastery in weaving multiple themes together, and she explores morality, justice, and mystery as the centrepieces of all her novels intermingled with exemplary storytelling finesse. Themes of justice, morality, and intrigue do not go unnoticed in Christie's novels. They often feature characters grappling with moral conflicts, revealing a Christie who understands human nature. These characters frequently tiptoe around ethical boundaries, engaging the readers deeply. Every one of her books is masterfully woven around a distinct enigma designed to captivate readers' attention and transport them into Christie's vibrant imagination. The readers follow the protagonist's moral compass through challenging puzzles and are left free to examine their own beliefs and values. Christie's novels are not merely murder mysteries; they compel one to analyse the intricacies of a society's moral framework and seek answers to questions like what drives morality and the consequences it has on human life.

Christie's works haven't aged a single day and are equally relatable across generations and cultures. Contemporary audiences are still fascinated by her criticisms of morality and justice intertwined with ageless perspectives on the human experience.

Her contributions to the literary world will always be remembered as compelling pieces of storytelling because of how expertly she intertwines the central themes of each work.

A Comparison With Contemporary Authors

Agatha Christie is a hallmark figure in crime fiction and one of the most prolific authors in literary history. The influence of her work stretches across different times and genres; within contemporary literature, it is common for authors to draw inspiration from Christie's novels. Her books are known for garnering immense popularity even after several years for which they were written and rarely received fame during her lifetime.

While reading modern works of crime fiction, Christie's influence can be seen in the novels of today's authors, who, like Christie, use intricate plot designs and elevated character development. From Tana French to Gillian Flynn to Paula Hawkins, Christie's classic novels, filled with intense suspense and ingenious plots, have influenced many contemporary authors, and they will continue to do so in the future.

Furthermore, the enduring popularity of Christie's iconic detectives, Hercule Poirot and Miss Marple, has enabled her successors in contemporary literature to create a new breed of detectives. Contemporary mystery writers like Louise Penny and Robert Galbraith (a pseudonym for J.K. Rowling) have incorporated Christie's famous detectives into their works, presenting new ways for audiences to solve baffling mysteries.

Christie's influence is not limited to classic crime fiction; her contribution to the emerging sub-genre of domestic noir is exemplified by Liane Moriarty and Shari Lapena, who deftly examine the sinister undercurrents of relationships enveloped within the façade of domestic tranquillity. This connection resonates with Christie's study of human nature and society, illustrating her extensive impact on modern writers.

In exploring the landscape of modern crime fiction, it is evident that Christie's exceptional artistry continues to influence new authors, shaping their writing with intellect and complexity. The familiar appeal of her characters, the intricacy of her plots, and the enduring artistry of her narrative have always provided hope and inspiration to help readers navigate the artful mazes of mystery and suspense in the contemporary world.

Reader Captivation: Crossing Generations and Cultures

The allure of Agatha Christie's writing is remarkable, withstanding the test of time and captivating readers from different cultures, regions, and generations. The ever-increasing resonance of her books has made Christie a miraculous phenomenon of literature, her superb storytelling and mastery of gripping narratives prevalent from the post-World War I era to the present era of technological advancement. Her writings require intellectual engagement and provide gratifying emotional involvement, showcasing plots rich in complexity, dynamic, multifaceted characters, and profound themes. Not for anything is audiences across the globe connected with her works. Adding to her appeal, Christie's stories' portrayal of human struggles and moral dilemmas is relatable and engaging, inspiring readers from all cultures and deepening their understanding of the world's complexities. This astounding cultural relevance proves Christie's remarkable understanding of humanity, having the ability to dive into the heart of the matter beyond age and societal boundaries. Like other great novelists, Christie has great skill in navigating psychological intricacies and moral ambiguities, aligning them with the quest for meaning and justice everyone seeks, making her work impactful for readers from all walks of life.

In addition, the numerous translations of her works show their appeal and adaptability to various cultural contexts. Her stories have been accepted globally, crossing cultural boundaries, which proves that they can stir intrigue, suspense, and deep thought no matter how different the culture is. The fact that people from different civilisations and Christie's captivating literature inspire and unify people is a testament to her legacy, which will continue to be told for generations to come.

Critical Appreciation and Scholarly Critiques

Christie's impact on literature is unmatched as it has received critical praise, fostering scholarly perspectives that further analyse her works. Literary experts and critics have invested time into Christie's storytelling, analysing her plots, characters, and themes. Christie's work has received praise for the complexity of her plots, the multifaceted development of her characters, and the profound societal critique comment incorporated into them. Her critics appreciate the way she captivates countless readers through her captivating plots and their entangling puzzles. She offers absorbing viewpoints on human nature and behaviour through her characters, which critically fascinates scholars who probe into the layers in her text. Also, the sociocultural commentary within her stories and the rich nuances of the period she wrote make them timeless, adding to scholarly discourse. Christie's works' adaptation, translation, and reinterpretation offer a broadened spectrum of multidisciplinary discourse, showcasing that her impact stretches beyond literature. Christie's adaptations into stage plays, films, and television shows have examined the blending of literature with other media types. These adaptations have examined the portrayal of Christie's works in different cultures and the accompanying translation processes. The Christie phenomenon in various international contexts reaffirms her novels' universal appeal in different languages. Christie's influence continues to spark academic debate around the issue of gender, ethical representation, and literary detectives. Active debates have centred on the depiction of gender relations in Christie's work, the ethical boundaries of justice and order in her stories, and the evolving identity of the detective in the stories. These debates have demonstrated the importance of Christie's work and her impact in the sphere of crime stories and literature. In summary, the enduring praise and analysis from critics and researchers highlights the profound impact of Agatha Christie and her fiction on crime literature.

While continuing to capture the interest of new generations

of readers and scholars, the depth and breadth of Christie's impact on the literary landscape remains a captivating vehicle for scholarly inquiry.

Setting the Stage for a Journey Through Her World

While experiencing a literary pilgrimage, readers step into the world of Agatha Christie, where vividly crafted characters are portrayed in intricate plots. In Christie's world, readers travel through alleys of suspense, psychological shadows, and the fine lines of morality and justice. The captivating nature of Christie's masterpieces, alongside her unparalleled storytelling, has intrigued audiences for generations, showcasing her literary marvel.

Moreover, the locations known from Christie's works are just as important as the characters of her stories. From the lavish drawing rooms of English country houses to the exotic places in the Middle East, every location acts as a stage where the drama occurs. Each description of the setting showcases attention to detail, which adds to the richness of the setting, evoking a vivid sense of place which charms the readers and ensnares the reader's imagination. Through her masterful prose, Christie enables her readers to travel these different landscapes, allowing them to solve mysteries in her meticulously crafted environments.

While travelling through the worlds Christie created, readers encounter a complex tapestry of societal standards fused with human behaviour.

Christie's narratives are equally accurate windows into the attitudes and social norms of the periods in which her stories take place. She explores the dynamics of social class, gender, and social networks, providing readers with timeless stories relevant to an array of cultures. Her keen understanding of human behaviour allows individuals within contemporary or historical society to be analysed and reflected upon.

In addition, the setting in which the stories take place is barren to the context of the characters, making them feel more tailored to the world in which they exist. The setting and the characters work in tandem to create a world where one impacts the other, all contributing to telling the story with precision. Christie meticulously designs a world that offers boundless exploration, drawing the reader into her stunning universe and bending the traditional definitions of storytelling.

2

Formative Years

Torquay to the First Tale

The Enchanted Childhood in Devon

As the English Riviera was being developed, it served as the architectural wonder's inspiration, hosting her something reminiscent of Europe's greatest works of art. This entire coastline certainly had the perfect place for any child to grow, and for her, as an aspiring author, the scenery offered immense potential that Torquay alone could not contain. With its warm climate, parts of Devon offered steep, jagged cliffs alongside crystal clear azure seas surrounded by vibrant vegetation. It is not an understatement that shrubby Torquay chronicles the effortless imagination that was to fuel the dreams of Comiti-Portba's vivid narrative Declawed. This travelogue was Porter's Gateway in Grande.

As the breathtaking elements of nature offered a plethora of possibilities to an aspiring author, it is clear that it alone allows Torquay to achieve remaining sublime things in life, for a child-bred imagination south of Loch Killaroo their South to diving using naturally luxurious electric blue basins.

Everything described immediately opens up so many ideas, and as vivid as this is, muddled words make a child's mind easily go far beyond the earthly realm that is full of dreaming seeds. This environment is simply perfect, and most importantly, establishing the beginnings of a great era for depth exploration gives real-world balance.

Novels based on enchantment, Gate Torquay crafted along-port, truly inspired the most defining era of Agatha. This also led the author to birth so many South ground Mer worded than a shy child who can touch.

A Fascination with Literature and Storytelling

Growing up in Torquay, Agatha Christie was surrounded by literature and storytelling from an early age. She loved reading a wide variety of books, from works of classic fiction to exciting detective stories. These books' elaborate plots and wonderful characters captured her imagination and sparked her interest in storytelling.

As she immersed herself in literature, Christie began noticing patterns and structures of plots with a particular form. This demonstrated the subtlety of plot progression and character development that became her hallmark later, sharpening with every word she penned. Her interest in human behaviour, along with its numerous deceiving masks, gave direction to her thoughts, which inspired her works.

Additionally, the books and stories her imagination could conjure enabled her to visit countless worlds beyond her own and instilled a wanderlust that could not be appeased. Her early access to various places and cultures fuelled her imagination, paving the way for the rich and exotic settings that would later form the gems of her literary pieces.

Unlike many, Christie was captivated from a young age. As such, her attention was drawn to clever mysteries and intricately woven storylines, which helped her gain a strong understanding of relationships among plots, characters, and settings in novels. She developed a keen eye for detail as she read different genres, paying attention to the works of world-famous authors and revelling in the mysteries.

Her love for literature and stories didn't end after her teenage years. Christie's passion for literature propelled her forward, reshaping her outlook on life while nurturing the writer deep within her. She realised the unparalleled impact literature can offer on both the reader and the writer, which shaped her into becoming one of the most well-known writers of the 20th century.

A Complex Family Dynamic and Its Influence

Agatha Christie's family had a notable impact on her life due to the characteristics Christie's family had. Every member of her family and their relations with each other formed a very rich tapestry which influenced the young Christie in one way or another. Her mother, Clara, was a fervently ambitious socialite, which did not hinder Agatha from developing a sense of independence. On the other hand, Frederick, her father, was very genial, and his warm nature enhanced Agatha's powers of watching and studying human behaviour, which was very helpful for her as a writer later on. Losing her father at the very young age of 11 impacted her deeply, and looking at loss and other dominating themes like grief and resilience later in life became strongly relatable for her through her literary works. The presence of elder siblings also proved essential for Agatha's formation because they came from differing worldviews, and their shared imaginative play fostered creativity. Agatha's storytelling capabilities were discovered and fostered by her older sister, Madge, who proved very supportive.

The dynamics of Agatha Christie's family life, with its peculiarities and subtleties, helped develop her ability to create complex characters and intricate social relationships that she later depicted in her writings. Throughout her life, Agatha's keen eye for detail was polished as she immersed herself within the delicate web of human emotions, interactions, families, and behaviours. As a result, she could depict human nature realistically, and this feature of her works delighted many people worldwide. The impact that her family relationships had on her was profound, especially evident in the literary works of Agatha Christie, which exhibit an extraordinary understanding of human nature and rich narratives.

Educational Pursuits: Formal and Otherwise

Agatha Christie's learning pursuits were as eclectic as the characters in her novels. Although she did not receive a formal education as a child, she used alternative resources, such as novels, to learn. As a child and even later, Agatha possessed an insatiable curiosity and followed her interests outside the boundaries of self-guided exploration and informal academic study. Even in what little form of schooling she went through, she was taught the basics outlined in standardised curricula, which got her started, but her unfettered need for knowledge could and did not rest easy with that.

Come adulthood, her circumstances brought self-restraint and limits; she became a self-taught expert on Literature, History, and even Philosophy due to her obsessive-compulsive nature. This unorthodox method of approaching education encouraged Agatha to explore newer realms of knowledge and integrate them into her behavioural studies and observations made over the years, which in turn made her writing richer. Agatha's exposure to an abundance of different fields of study early on greatly enhanced her understanding of fiction writing and prepared her for her future literary work.

Together with her academic pursuits, Agatha Christie's travels and interactions with different peoples and cultures expanded her insights more than anything else. Being exposed to different environments, including thinking patterns, customs, and belief systems, added to her appreciation of humanity. As such, these factors fueled her imagination and endowed her with remarkable powers of observation and insight—markers of her creativity.

These striking trends shaped Christie's life as an unconventional learner, setting her on a trajectory that would change storytelling paradigms while ensuring a deeper understanding of human nature. Her unique scholarly journey and astute engagement with people positioned her for the eventual mark she would forge in literature, ultimately establishing her reputation as the Queen of Crime.

Early Inspirations: Influences of Genre and Authors

Inspired by various genres and authors, Agatha Christie's early life was characterised by an uncontrollable passion for reading. The sophisticated tales of Edgar Allan Poe delighted her with mysteries shrouded in ever-darkening arias, as did the spine-tingling Sherlock Holmes depicted by Sir Arthur Conan Doyle and P.G. Wodehouse's witty narratives. All of the above authors influenced Agatha Christie as a child and are what can be termed the first stepping stone of her liking for literature. Wilkie Collins and Mary Elizabeth Braddon are equally gripping and brilliant Victorian novelists with remarkable, intricate tale weaving, and Christie's deep admiration for secrets—their intertwining- propelled the vivid imagination the world knows her for today. Dorothy L. Sayers' and Anthony Berkeley's works, still captivating, are golden-age whodunnits, which gave her interest in drama construction and duplicitous deception and plot.

As her literary palette broadened its boundaries, all these early influences blended and sculpted the groundwork of her future undertakings. Christie's voracious reading habits across numerous genres not only exercised her imagination but also equipped her with essential knowledge about the craft of storytelling, character creation, and plotting. These works of literature during her formative years essayed the role of guiding stars to assist her on her way to becoming a remarkable author and ultimately achieving her title as the Queen of Crime.

The First Experiments with Writing

With the development of Agatha Christie's life came a fierce curiosity that relished exploring the realms of writing. She had a vivid imagination as an early child, and her use of literature everywhere makes it clear that the girl also loved books. During this period, she started writing poems and short stories, first as a challenge to express herself and later to let her creativity flow. With each write-up, she strived to perfect her craft. Every work became a stepping stone to refine her skills to flawless beauty. In her earlier work, she tried to depict complicated plots filled with deep character analysis while exploring Christie's fascinating emotions as she strove to grasp the human experience through prose. Agatha Christie's earliest writings that piqued her interest in mystery and suspense became the catalyst for her enigmatic career-defining narrative fiction. In her earlier works, she began understanding the importance of storytelling, pacing, emotion and withholding information in refining her writing.

The primary attempts at innovation by the budding writer strayed from convention, proving fertile ground for the unparalleled originality that would come to define her artistic masterpieces. Even at these early stages, it was inevitable that Christie's voice and storytelling would develop into something that eventually the world was bound to call for. Christie's writing experiences can be viewed as a crucible from which her legacy was born because in them lay the strength of devotion and determination towards achieving literary immortality.

The Blossoming of a Curious Mind

Christie's exploration of literary and artistic landscapes was accompanied by an insatiable curiosity for music, archaeology, and even deeper philosophical exploration. All of this equipped her to weave intricate plots and compelling characters that could be created only by drawing inspiration ensconced in human nature. Bringing new perspectives, themes, and ideas into her writing made it mouth-watering for readers.

Christie's unquenchable thirst for knowledge from ancient civilisations to contemporary philosophies made her delve into every possible study area. As she absorbed new societies and cultures, her interactions informed her storytelling, psychology, and culture, enhancing the authenticity of her narratives. Such an immersive approach to learning cultivated an unrivalled depth and insight in her work as a novelist.

In addition, Christie's reading habits were equally eclectic. Her voracious appetite for reading exposed her to many literary styles and genres, honing her imagination and nurturing her creativity. She digested everything in her path, from classical works to contemporary books, effectively moulding her writing style. This diverse literary diet formed the underpinning of her future accomplishments as she skillfully incorporated different storytelling traditions into her celebrated body of work.

Her interest in psychology, human behaviour, and the finer details of human emotion and interaction was striking for an emerging writer. Her deeper understanding of human behaviour at that point enabled her to give life to rich, profound, and diverse characters in her novels. This deep comprehension of humanity and society made narratives that would appeal to readers from different age groups possible.

The childhood curiosity of Agatha Christie contributed significantly towards her evolution as an author, but it doesn't stop there; it is also the reason behind the timelessness of her works. With such an understanding of human nature and an unquenchable thirst for acquiring more knowledge, she was always bound to create something far too deep and complex. Ultimately, this is how she transformed into a revered author for ages.

Personal Hardships and Their Impact on Creativity

Charles's romance did not greatly spoil Christie's life. The open envelope sent to Agatha containing her treasured father's images was game-changing for her. It triggered her psychological problems, such as having a heavy hammer-like head, which abandoned her at 11; she went through the social protocol to raise a child while also accepting traditional views. Moreover, the same images, with socially induced grief masked by abandonment, may not have led her towards pole psychology, emotional reflection, and human intricacies, which later in life gave her the ability to explore missing pieces of the equation as well. In addition, her nursing experiences during the world war and later disguising herself as a father who dispensed medicine exposed the hidden curtains towards suffering. The attending nurses, with their aid, were likely responsible for the worst human condition injuries. There is no doubt that these problems, while alive, nurtured patriotism unrivalled within people, along with her understanding of psychology, crime, and humanity simultaneously. Alongside pain, relentless passive encouragement fuelled determination but also mental insanity, shaping boundless compassion for countless struggling individuals.

Agatha Christie's writing creativity was deeply affected by her early life struggles. She continues to captivate audiences by transforming her challenges into compelling, timeless stories.

Support and Encouragement from Family

Agatha Christie's life as a writer was extremely focused on family, and she relied on their unwavering support and motivation. Even during trying times, such as losing her father at an early age and going through a difficult first marriage, Agatha was able to draw strength from the love and compassion surrounding her. Clara, her mother, nurtured Agatha's imagination by acquiring many literature and storytelling books, which helped expand her horizons. As a result, Agatha was raised in a family that appreciated art and was actively curious about various domains. Such an environment changed Agatha's perspective of the world and prepared her for future great literary successes. During her growing years, Agatha's family provided her with a protective bubble away from external stressors, which helped her focus on writing. Along with enabling her writing, this support from her family stemmed from the belief that Agatha had immense talent and was capable of reaching great heights. Her family understood her amazing ability to engage people with captivating stories and made sure she could choose writing as a career without hurdles.

The steadfast belief in her capabilities undoubtedly strengthened Agatha's resolve and fuelled her ambition to pursue a career as a novelist. Furthermore, their active participation, especially during moments of despair or lack of inspiration, kept her motivated and emotionally grounded. Her connection with her family enabled Agatha to incorporate authenticity and deep emotional resonance into her work. Her rich life experiences and understanding of her familial relationships inspired her. In any case, the firm support and encouragement from her family turned Agatha Christie into a masterful writer for myriad readers even now, decades after her passing.

Draft of Destiny: Crafting Her First Manuscript

Agatha Christie's journey towards becoming one of the most celebrated mystery writers of all time began with the first manuscript she single-handedly wrote. The initial draft of her first transformative manuscript was not a mere happenstance but a culmination of endless experiences, influences, inspirations, and the grit she exhibited. Even when Agatha was young, she possessed an appetite for remarkable stories. Thus, with the unfettered support from her family, she indulged in deep literary explorations and thinking. This circles back to the fact that Agatha's first manuscript was a product of her family's nurturance.

Awash with imagination related to intricate plots, unfurling complexities of humankind, and ageless mysteries waiting to be solved, Christie's introspective odyssey became a reality. The central strategies that shaped the characters, settings, and story that would later bolster her legacy required rigorous attention to detail and an unrelenting commitment to perfection.

The beginning of Christie's first manuscript was both a passion project and a saga filled with challenges and accomplishments. It showcased her persistence in bringing her imagination to the pages and is a testament to her skills as an emerging author. The manuscript is a tribute to her crafting captivating narratives that engage the intellect and evoke deep emotions.

In her search for creativity, Agatha leveraged the spirit of her bygone years, drawing from the rich emotional depths of her youth, which profoundly shaped her inspirations. Every word written was an enlightenment, and every character created was designed to add texture to the story. Each sentence blended her effort and unwavering determination to make her dreams a reality.

Within her writing sanctuary, she battled doubt and emerged victorious with a manuscript representing the triumph of her dreams and abilities. Completing her first manuscript was a cornerstone in her life. It showcased her undying spirit, resolute demeanour, and unwavering commitment to achieving excellence in writing. This document captured the complete form of her creative journey and was the foundation of the unmatched legacy she intended to produce in the following years.

3

The Birth of a Genre

Early Works and Breakthroughs

Overview: The Golden Age of Detective Fiction

The Golden Age of Detective Fiction, a period that dawned in the early 20th century, continues to enthrall readers with its timeless mysteries. This era, which saw the rise of detective novels, established conventions that have stood the test of time. At its heart were astonishingly intricate plots, phenomenal storytelling, and characters that remain as fresh and engaging as they were when they first graced the pages.

The most notable element of the Golden Age was storytelling through the articulation of complex mysteries and cunning sleuthing. Writers during this era carefully crafted elaborate plots alongside cleverly nuanced red herrings. This period also highly revered the typical whodunit formula in which the perpetrator is kept a guarded secret until the final moment, revealing a heart-racing moment of ecstasy for the reader.

The Golden Age of Detective Fiction is one of the most significant periods in classic fiction. From Hercule Poirot to Sherlock Holmes, readers were presented with an array of relentless sleuths, each with their unique spin on deduction. Characters such as those created by Agatha and Arthur have become household names and epitomes for an entire genre rooted in mystery.

The setting in these stories was intertwined with post-war society, offering a completely different narrative than what is offered today. A mixture of economic revitalisation paired with changes in social norms provided a new lens for readers. The broadness of the context, coupled with the rich plot, added an unprecedented level of depth, resonance, and exploration that no classic fiction offered.

The Golden Age of Detective Fiction, far from being a mere source of entertainment, sparked a wave of curiosity that continues to ripple through the literary world. Its influence on subsequent generations of writers is undeniable, as it prompted them to delve deeper into the realms of content, morality, and human nature. In the following chapters, we will delve into the works, influence, and legacy of the Golden Age literature, celebrating its profound impact on the world of literature.

`The Mysterious Affair At Styles: Agatha's Debut`

The novel sets the stage in the centre of World War I and adds a helpful touch by exploiting all the confusion and uncertainty surrounding the war to create a factor of intrigue and thrilling suspense. In Agatha Christie's `The Mysterious Affair at Styles,' readers were introduced to a somewhat different type of detective story that was unlike what had been published at the time.

This story was well known for introducing Hercule Poirot, an inspired Belgian detective whose extreme attention to detail, great intelligence, and eccentric manners played a critical part in the story. For the first time, Christie gave the genre of detective stories a new perspective and shifted the focus from hardboiled detectives. For Christie, this was the kickoff of an unparalleled career and the debut of an iconic character worldwide. Hercule is still famous in the modern world. The artist's meticulous work provided in this book, like classic detective complex plots, red herrings, and intricate storytelling, ensured people wanted to commission her for another book the moment the first one was published.

Crafting a Signature Style: Early Influences and Techniques

In her early years of writing, Agatha Christie carefully developed a distinctive style of writing that made her a household name and a leader in detective fiction. Christie was unique in structuring stories with complicated plots and astonishing psychological elements. Set pieces like her Meridian Pharmacy were also informative to a fictional character's transformation, inferring that one's own mind's workplace stimulated imaginations through wartime occupations, such as being a dispensing chemist during World War I. Christie's understanding of human nature was a remarkable tool that added an air of authenticity and depth to her characters. Social studies aside, Christie's childhood passion for the natural sciences and archaeology provided her with a clue to structure reasoning and a great eye for appreciating detail, which was reflected in the tightness of her plot construction and results-driven unravelling of mysteries.

The impacts of the traditional English backdrop and the refined culture of the interwar period also influenced her writing, incorporating traces of time and location that engrossed her readers in an incredible world. Furthermore, her passion for the genre fuelled her exploration of different plot designs and methods of narration, further establishing her reputation as a skilled writer in the developing field of detective fiction. This was the framework from which Agatha Christie's style erupted, combining discernment and scientific rigour with human understanding. While refining her art, she cultivated a dependable voice, gaining favourable critiques and establishing her enduring impact on literature.

Critical Reception: Embracing the New Literary Star

Agatha Christie's entrance into the literary world with 'The Mysterious Affair at Styles' received praise, admiration, and innovative criticism. As a debuting author in the Golden Age of Detective Fiction, Christie's early writings were noted not just for their captivating plots but also for attention to detail alongside character development. Both the public and critics were not shy in showing that there was a serious contender in the literary space, acknowledging her unique talent for building plots that kept her readers yearning for more. Christie's rise as a female writer in an era where male authors dominated the literary scene was a highlight because it added to Christie's works' impact and her own. Her astonishing crime fiction works shocked readers and changed the paradigms of the genre. Reviews of her early works frequently appreciated her for the refreshing take she presented on the genre through complex puzzles intertwined with drama. The depth of Christie's complex characters and eloquent plot-spin masters were equally regarded by the critics, who some claimed were spellbound by her.

In addition, her remarkable insight into social class and human everyday life added to the nuance of her stories, which were loved far and wide. Each subsequent publication drew increasing attention to Christie as a literary star, admired for her ingenious and skilful narratives of captivating puzzles. Smaller stories evolved into larger written masterpieces, further increasing her popularity and solidifying her cherished reputation among readers. Reviews of her early works showcased the recognition Christie was starting to receive as a great storyteller and illustrated the beginning of a legacy that attracted readers from many eras. The affectionate reception of Agatha Christie's works by the public and discerning critics initiated her career and unlocked doors to redefining detective fiction, earning her a respectable name in literature.

Character Innovation: Birth of Hercule Poirot

Hercule Poirot, a name that would echo through literary history, was the invention of Agatha Christie. Christie's Poirot changed the expectations of detectives in literature. His attention to detail and neurotic self-descriptions of "little grey cells" made him stand out. Described as an immaculately dressed and slow-paced Belgian detective, Poirot's character was loved by readers.

Christie's approach to designing characters for her work was innovative, as was every work featuring Poirot. His precision and fastidious grooming habits made him relatable, which in turn made him popular everywhere. Pouring all her creativity into one character ensured his mannerisms would be loved globally. Starting with a foreign character as the protagonist set new standards in the genre and presented a new form of perception to detective novels.

The development of Poirot's character illustrates the evolution of the people surrounding him and the great intellect we know to be Poirot himself. While other authors prioritised raw intellect in their characters, Christie implemented a unique and multi-faceted approach that followed the telling of what was now called 'The Great War'. Virtually, as the war swept over Europe, the Belgian Detective saw himself as a symbol of order. The astonishing insights he displayed while unravelling the sometimes-tangled web of human nature, society, and social norms created a case for him as the finest detective to have ever walked the planet. Throughout time, his uncanny yet jocular ways of dealing with people made readers fall in love with him. Surely, Poirot was not a man of wonders but was a benchmark for personas that emerged in crime fiction novels.

Moreover, Poirot's evolution throughout the series mirrors Christie's growth as a writer. In addition, his character is solidified by Agatha Christie's astounding intelligence. Poirot underwent various developments with each novel, but with every change, Christie's genius was highlighted. This is fundamentally true due to the baffling elegance with which Christie blended Poirot's traits postulated by humans and unparalleled accuracy as a detective. Therefore, even his persona, which was crafted by bringing straightforwardness rather than depth, jellied readers across the globe.

With the creation of Hercule Poirot, a unique and elaborate character quite unlike anything seen before, Agatha Christie forever shaped the mystery fiction world. Christie's literature has changed the world's cultural landscape and remains popular today.

Trailblazing Challenges: Gender Dynamics in Publishing

During the early 20th century, the publishing industry was a 'man's world', a reflection of the societal gender dynamics that greatly influenced the hurdles and opportunities for aspiring women writers like Agatha Christie. In this context, women's voices were, at best, marginalised in the industry's power structure, and women's roles and expectations within it were greatly straitjacketed. Agatha's experiences highlight the shifting paradigms regarding women's roles in literature. Despite such barriers, Agatha remained determined, faced dauntless challenges, and made tremendous strides in the industry. Her remarkable fortitude transformed the detective fiction genre and the pathways for women writers to come. Agatha's triumphs were a significant milestone in the journey of women's empowerment in and around the publishing domain. She inspired many women to cultivate their entrepreneurial spirit. Instead, this woman shouldered the burden of her legacy and guided women to write without hesitation, no matter what constraining borders of society define them.

The example set forth by Agatha Christie reminds us of the

impact that relentless people can have while changing the gender balance in literature. Christie's life sheds light on the struggles and triumphs of her life and highlights how she fought for gender-related inequalities in literature during her time.

Notable Works and Their Impact: A Chronological Perspective

Christie achieved a remarkable career lasting over six decades and authored numerous works that fundamentally changed the mystery genre. Her first novels, The Mysterious Affair at Styles and The Secret Adversary, were above and beyond owing to their complex reasons and suspenseful nature. These works prepared the reader for Christie's literary approach while making her an authoritative figure within the literary universe. Christie did not stop there and continued to famously surprise audiences with her later works like Murder on the Orient Express, Death on The Nile, and And Then There Were None. With each of them, Christie showed her readers her ability to construct intricate plots, complex personas and multiple sub-plots for each diabolical twist she included. A clear example is Murder on the Orient Express, where the audience is used to the morally righteous ending only to be left in anguish right after the climax. With Death on the Nile, the author used the overabundance of foreign touristic locations to their full advantage by fully incorporating them into the context of the plot.

Christie's masterpiece, 'And Then There Were None', exemplifies her ability to blend psychological suspense with ethical conflicts, serving as a testament to her unrivalled genius. Christie's literary prowess evolved with each new release, marking her as a trailblazer in crime fiction. Furthermore, her short stories featuring characters like Miss Marple and Hercule Poirot enriched her legacy. In addition, Christie's influence went beyond the pages of books as her novels were adapted for the stage, films, and television. The lasting importance of her works is that they can appeal to people from different eras and continue to be loved by readers around the globe. Exploring Christie's significant works chronologically allows us to understand her phenomenal contributions to literature better and further appreciate her status as the undisputed royalty of crime fiction.

Literary Partnerships and Collaborations

As much as Agatha Christie's career as a writer is characterised by her achievements, it is equally defined by her collaborations and partnerships with other authors and professionals within the industry. Throughout her career, Christie participated in several collaborative ventures that expanded her writing horizons and added greater depth to her work. One of her most memorable collaborations was with Sir Arthur Conan Doyle, the man behind Sherlock Holmes. The union of these two literary titans saw the coming together of Hercule Poirot and Sherlock Holmes in 'The Adventure of the Christmas Pudding,' described in a short story competition between the two. This partnership was the first of its kind. It fused two literary detectives from different worlds for the first time and was a treat to the readers of both authors. Moreover, Christie's association with notable playwrights like Agatha Christie and Josephine Tey brought about successful adaptations of her works for the stage. Their mastery as writers for the theatre was a perfect complement to Christie's intricate prose and exquisite storytelling, resulting in masterpieces that still capture audiences across the globe. Further, Christie's pioneering partnerships went beyond the creative circle to her publishers and editors, expanding her reach and collaborating with refined professionals. By working closely with the publishing team at William Collins & Sons (now HarperCollins), she was able to improve her manuscripts, devise new marketing approaches, and expand her audience. Author and publisher symmetry aided in Christie's living legacy and the continuing success of her literary works. A further contribution of Christie's is her collaboration with illustrators and cover artists, which helped define her works' overarching aesthetic. These partnerships, including the iconic dust jackets and character depictions, enhanced the reading experience and transformed her novels into collectables. In other words, Agatha Christie's sustained creativity with other writers and industry professionals engaged her in ways that improved the literary world. She pioneered what it means to rely on many different creative people to tell inspiring stories and changed the world's perspective on literature.

Refining the Mystery Formula: Continuous Evolution

During Agatha Christie's writing career, she adapted and improved the mystery genre, which has had a lasting impact on literature. The evolution of her style showcased her writing, plot design, and character development, signifying that she was always seeking perfection. Christie painstakingly crafted her work with elaborate clues alongside misleading clues within clues that kept readers engaged in her unrivalled puzzles. She had an unrivalled talent for balancing critical complexity and basic understandability, something that perpetuates her relevance today. This masterful story composition, paired with her experimentation with point of view, added layers to the narrative, building intrigue and solidifying her place in literary mastery.

In addition, the range of locations and themes that Christie tackled changed the landscape for modern detective fiction. From dull English towns to vibrant new locations, her imagination and ability to "paint with words" greatly enhanced her storytelling and set the stage for complex mysteries. In addition, themes such as human psychology, morality, social structure, and many more advanced ideas made her stories resonate with readers, young and old. The relentless change in Christie's mystery formula showed her flexibility and willingness to explore new frontiers in the genre. She skillfully adapted to changes in the rest of literature by incorporating modern elements into classic whodunits. While embracing societal changes and technological advancements, the essence of her timeless storytelling remained intact.

Additionally, Christie's attention to character development set a higher bar for the genre. Including Hercule Poirot and Miss Marple as her central detectives, Christie's protagonists underwent a remarkable and complex evolution beyond the mere change expected of a detective. Readers could deepen their connection with these complex figures as they grappled with challenges and underwent change in each instalment.

In summary, Christie's cunning set the groundwork for the current genre through her pursuit of perfecting her mystery formula and evolving her storytelling. 'The Agatha Christie and 'The Queen of Crime' change what the rest of the world will deem necessary in the past. Her unwavering innovation and blending of tradition led to her unforgivable legacy in the genre.

Final Remarks: Building a Legacy

After analysing Agatha Christie's work and milestones, it becomes clear that her absolute devotion to mystery fiction has profoundly impacted its linear history. Her legacy is built upon the evolving structure of mystery novels. Christie's craft, blending captivating characters, intricate plots, and suspense-filled narratives, continues shaping the literary industry.

Christie's inspiration goes beyond her written spins, affecting the general public, a multitude of writers, directors, and fans. Throughout her writing career, a blend of intellect and creativity allowed her to surpass existing boundaries of detective stories and set new landmarks that writers still aim for today.

In addition to her written work, Christie has succeeded in defining social and cultural norms, showcasing the presence of her legacy. Her storytelling has enabled her to walk through complex themes and societal details while redefining human perception with a profound lens and deep insights. The beauty of her work is that it can be enjoyed at any time.

Christie's legacy is almost synonymous with Hercule Poirot and Miss Marple, and it is difficult to separate her work from the pop culture impact of these characters. People around the world recognise and remember them as exemplary figures of detection, intelligence, and unwavering resolve. Their existence in Christie's works not only catered to the entertainment appetite of her followers but also educated them about human nature and morality.

It is widely known that Christie was and remains unrivalled in mystery literature, and her works are timeless. Her works are an amalgamation of fiction, literary mastery, and cultural subtleties, making her unique. The fact that her readers have not exhausted her works to the present proves that exploring Christie's works fuels curiosity and imagination, encouraging her audience to indulge in self-reflection.

In a way, Agatha Christie's earlier works and accomplishments continue to be guiding milestones for subsequent authors and readers. Her contributions to the literary world show us the fascination behind mysteries, the art of weaving tales, and boundless human imagination. In Christie's masterpieces, she leads us to enigmatic worlds where secrets are buried, waiting to be uncovered.

4
Unraveling Intricacies

Deception and Human Psychology in Her Work

Introduction to Christie's Psychological Layers

Christie achieves masterful writing through the multifaceted exploration and application of motive psychology, which, with remarkable insight, is reflected in her works. Psychology never eluded her; she captured it through forensic detail, receiving merit acclaim for her craft that never witnessed idle stagnation. In every story, intricate designs of crime and irrationality capture us to become learners of new definitions of thought. The psychology behind motives and crime takes one's breath away through every intelligent construction. We, the readers, are travellers in the world created by Agatha, where her astonishing ability to put pen to paper spins motives into suspicion on mysterious roads interwoven with the glamour of reasoning. Agatha showcased both medicine and poultice of emulation and self-scepticism, shedding light on the depths of self admonished through the prism of multi-level deception, which encapsulates boundaries around deep intricacy that lie dead at first sight. Each character pushes the envelope of psychology while the underlying sentiment captures the feeling of expectation united towards one goal, admonished through the crafted narrative that disintegrates prior defined norms.

Moreover, Christie's nuanced exploration of the trauma's effect on memory and the construction of space and identity adds profound depth to her narratives, setting them apart from ordinary crime fiction. By integrating such multi-dimensional psychological factors, Christie not only enchants her audience, but also presents the captivating bewilderments of human nature. Through her works, readers are invited to engage with the fundamental verities and confounding intricacies of human nature, sparking a sense of wonder and discovery. This is why this introduction is fitting for the rich exploration of the fascinating psychological nuances of Agatha Christie's literature.

Crafting Deception: Methods and Mechanisms

At the heart of Agatha Christie's greatness as a mystery writer is the art of deception. The techniques and devices that she constructed to create intricate webs of lies have permanently altered the genre. One of her major weapons is the alteration of perception, often achieved through the selective control of information. As Christie leads her readers through complex mazes of doubt and uncertainty, she reveals selective fragments of truths. This ensures the mystery's true essence is paradoxically obscured, yet astonishingly within reach. The sense of accomplishment when deciphering these webs of lies is a testament to Christie's skill and the reader's engagement.

Also, no one else does psychological or misdirection like Christie does. She describes people to the reader in a particular way, making it very likely that the reader will conclude well before all evidence has been presented. Only to have their conclusions subverted later, showcasing how misled we can be when we try to think too fast, and the reality is far more intricate. This designed guidance of the reader's perceptions and feelings adds more weight to the final fall, which the reader encounters, making them think deeply for some time after reading the last line.

A different example of Christie's skilful deception artistry is how she manages to change narrative perspective with so much skill. In every single piece, she cleverly uses unreliable or multiple narrators to hide the truth under which the story is wrapped in multiple layers of uncertainty. This intentional disturbance of clear discrepancy between truth and fiction makes the reader work hard to follow the story, inviting fresh strands of logic not bound by the confines of reason to find the truth.

In conjunction with the strategies already discussed, Christie seamlessly incorporates misdirection elements into her stories' physical aspects. Locations that initially seem quiet and comforting spiral into eerie and threatening places, and what seem to be banal objects might be crucial to solving the crime. These deeply planned contextual elements add another layer of spatial deception crafted by Christie's meticulous mind, illustrating her brilliance in manipulating the motives and perceptions of both the characters and the readers.

As a result, deception becomes an explicit motif in Christie's writings, showcasing not only Christie's wit in storytelling but also how deeply she comprehends the underlying concepts of the human mind. By taking such an approach, she puts her audience in a blend of reality and fantasy, only to navigate them towards differentiating the truth from lies, all submerged in complexity and riddles.

The Interplay of Truth and Illusion

The famous works of Agatha Christie ALWAYS emphasise the balance of truth and illusion as their central theme. Given the myriad layers and complexities involved, it is bound to make the audience think. Christie has a remarkable knack for writing stories that can blend reality with deception, which always mesmerises her audience with the understanding of the complexities of human psychology awash with reality. Every lie that Christie's characters weave leads to a whole new world of possibilities – this exploration, which is centred around the lies, shows how criminally deceptive things can appear and steer both the characters and readers off course. As always, Christie's mysteries cleverly capture the balancing act of truth and fiction through every single plot twist to explore how lies affect people and society.

In 'The Interplay of Truth and Illusion', one of the most profound reflections of misinterpretations and misplaced assumptions is assessed closely. Christie introduces readers to several characters caught up in lies and illusions through her stories. Along with this complexity, she exposes motives, intentions, and the fine line between perception and reality. Christie's storytelling invites readers to meander through intricate and bizarre cartoon landscapes while confronting their susceptibility to tricks, thus making readers ponder deeply.

In addition, "The Interplay of Truth and Illusion" acts as a starting point for exploring trust and doubt in a relationship. Christie's work shows how lies interfere and deepen folds even in the most genuine seeming interactions, resulting in the tearing of bonds of humanity. While doing so, the readers are forced to examine the notions of the frail certainties they thought to be reassuring and the level of strength required to stand in a world where reality and deception fight for control.

Balancing manifold facets of human psychology and ethical dilemmas, Christie's interweaving tales showcase the interplay of truth and deception regarding man's existence. 'The Interplay of Truth and Illusion' blends the essence of Christie's storytelling, serving as a reflective call to her audience to contemplate the meanings of truth, self, and the inescapable cycle of reality and pretence. In exploring the vivid landscapes of Christie's narratives, the readers undergo an introspective journey towards redefining their understanding of human nature, deception, and psychological depth—contemplating the delicate yet sturdy nature of truth wrapped within a deceitful world.

Profiling the Criminal Mind

Agatha Christie brought psychological analysis to her work in Christie's profiling and analysis of criminal behaviour. She has unique motives based on real-life humanistic tendencies. In her stories, she peeks under the skin of the outer layer of a criminal's psyche, examining one's childhood, upbringing, societal influences, and personal experiences that can shape one's inclination towards crime. By bringing forth the rationalisations and justifications of the antagonists, she compels her readers to think beyond the boundaries of law and morality in terms of crime, guilt, and redemption. Her works are extreme thrillers that glimpse humans' underlying nature. Moreover, Christie's criminals do not fall within ordinary and narrow-minded categories of people. She offers an extensive array of ill-minded people bound by separate reasons and motives that make them evil. Be it out of avarice, envy, or vengeance. The author constructs complex psychological portraits that unfurl powerful motives behind the antagonists' actions, making her characters believable.

This unique approach towards balancing the criminal psyche and blending realism into it marks Christie's novels as more than just ordinary whodunits, elevating them into remarkable explorations of human nature and deviance. She not only entertains and amazes her readers, but Christie also encourages readers to consider morality and empathy's fundamental questions by analysing the criminal psyche. All in all, the perceptive profiling of the criminal mind in Agatha Christie's work reflects her stunning mastery of unravelling the human psyche and implores the readers to consider the nature of wrongdoings and the vulnerability of the human mind.

Motives and Morality: The Ethical Dilemma

In Agatha Christie's intriguing works, the concept of motives and morality evolves into an arena full of puzzles to delve through. What lies at the epicentre of most of her novels is the oldest interrogative mind-bender of 'What drives a human being to commit crimes?', revealing the tangle of human psychology and moral reasoning. The depiction of characters dealing with the tempting yet dangerous aspect of their moral values indicates Christie's keen insights into the nature of humanity.

In addition, Christie's multidimensional motives within her plots reveal periods of psychological unravelling that reveal what drives people to take dangerous steps. Whether out of resentment, revenge, or jealousy, she makes it a point that readers grasp all the reasons that cause an individual to go beyond the boundaries set by society and what is considered moral.

The ethical dilemma is not solely restricted to the crimes mentioned above. The same applies to the detectives and even the readers. Christie brings the reader to the void spaces of one's morals and questions their actions through the ambiguity of specific settings, overcoming existing boundaries of right or wrong. Her purpose of complicating morality within her storytelling deepens its meaning, ultimately transcending her work beyond mere entertainment into thought-provoking contemplation regarding humanity.

In addition, exploring motives and ethical considerations blends the lines of fascinating storytelling with an astounding understanding of human behaviour. As Christie presents the complex nature of motive and morality, she gets the reader thinking about the psychological aspects of humanity. This stark comparison tends to appeal towards criminal activities and one's choices, combining factors that shape decisions and dilemmas that question one's humanity.

Ultimately, through investigating motives and morality, Agatha Christie weaves a profound web of ethical dilemmas that go beyond the bounds of her stories, deeply resonating with readers and inviting them to ponder the delicate interplay of motivations and moral judgment in the real world.

Psychological Manipulation: More than Just a Plot

In Agatha Christie's work, psychological manipulation is more than a plot device. It is a key element of her captivating storytelling. Christie's plots, with their characters, dialogues, and situations, are a testament to her deep understanding of human psychology. The narrative creates a troubling ambiguity around emotions, motivations, and perceptions, drawing the reader into an immersive experience that is both captivating and engrossing.

The blurring of lines regarding emotions, motivations, perceptions, and authenticity intricately reveals order masked by chaos. This is the essence of psychological manipulation. Christie's skillful construction of trust to guarantee betrayal leaves the reader intrigued, pondering the events unfolding as they seek to disentangle the web of chaos formed by Christie's manipulation.

Additionally, Christie's studies on psychological manipulation extend beyond the boundaries of mystery novels. She examines the depths of the human mind and uncovers the vulnerabilities that make a person open to influence. Her characters serve as pawns trapped in a psychologically precarious situation, underscoring the fragility of the human psyche and the remarkable ease with which it can be controlled.

Christie offers a compelling critique of the power dynamics in relationships through her keen understanding of behaviour and conditioning techniques. Whether using gentle influence, tactical intimidation, or emotional leverage, her characters employ psychological strategies that mirror authentic interactions, compelling readers to consider the extent of manipulation within society.

In other words, psychological manipulation within Agatha Christie's works goes beyond narrative strategies, revealing troubling aspects of human behaviour. It forces the readers to reflect upon the harsh truth of psychological exposure and nudges them into considering their ability to breach behavioural boundaries. Thus, Christie's manipulation of psychological elements transforms her works from simple entertainment into profound literature, marking her as a leading figure in the depths of psychological conversation.

Narrative Strategies: Red Herrings and Misdirection

A compelling mystery requires extensive character development and plotlines, but red herrings and misdirection must be utilised equally. It is known that Agatha Christie adored the genre and employed these strategies to charm her readers and captivate them until the text's conclusion. Red herrings are the breadcrumbs that lead the reader down false paths to misguide them, and misdirection is defined as taking attention away from the actual solution. Christie's plots relied on manipulating these elements to create suspense and intrigue. It is through red herrings and misdirection that Christie's superb planning and execution confuse and entertain readers. With her trademark style of red herrings and misdirection, Christie achieves a new level of mastery, precisely orchestrating how her audience is guided to solve the puzzle while being charmingly misinformed. The absolute best part for me was how she kept her audience misled yet captivated. From this perspective, the reader can be misled while looking and discerning the truth.

For instance, in 'The Murder of Roger Ackroyd', the identity of the murderer is cleverly concealed through the use of a red herring, leading the reader to suspect a different character. Similarly, in 'Murder on the Orient Express', Christie employs misdirection to divert attention from the true solution, creating a compelling and surprising narrative. The implementation of red herrings and misdirection enabled Christie to demonstrate her acute narrative craftsmanship by infusing life into her mysteries that required deep appreciation instead of mechanical solving. These features highlighted her acute psychological insight into readers and their nature's primal instincts. Christie's use of literary red herrings alongside misdirection fanned the flames of suspense and elevated the impact of surprises ensuring a gratifying resolution. This orchestration reinforces her reputation as a masterful suspense writer while deepening the fascination surrounding her work. Her sophisticated storytelling compels readers to engage with her works on multiple levels, revealing their timeless nature as Christie's artistry cleaves through the genres of crime and mystery. In-depth analysis demonstrates her brilliant skill in creating solid narrative structure wherein red herrings woven into the plot serve an elevated purpose as props that transcend literary boundaries, thereby establishing her succession as the unrivalled queen of crime.

Character Complexities: Beyond Good and Evil

Agatha Christie's works feature intricate characters that are neither straightforwardly good nor evil. Instead, they reflect a great balance and understanding of human nature. With her trademark style, she balances characters packed with contradictions and archetypes; whether redeeming or condemnable, Christie offers simplistic explorations of the human psyche.

Christie's protagonists and antagonists integrate a new structure regarding the system of morality, portraying good and evil characteristics. It is in the depiction of struggles within human beings, their fears, and aspirations that Christie casts a spell that portrays the weakness and strength of human beings. From the shrewd Hercule Poirot to the superficially simple Miss Marple, these characters are relatable in different contexts because they blend good and bad.

Moreover, Christie's characters go beyond mere plot devices; they articulate the intricate details of humanity. Their actions and motives compel readers to consider the ethical, behavioural, and societal complexities a person may face. The incompatibility of so many traits within one character is perhaps one of the most profound ways to scrutinise humanity's nature and complexity.

Furthermore, the good-versus-evil conflict is vividly

brought out through the interactions of the characters, enabling the audience to analyse the core struggle. Each clash showcases individual morality against the backdrop of surrounding realities, defying clear-cut dualities, and instead depicting a sophisticated density in moral confrontation. This 'sophisticated density' refers to the complex and nuanced nature of the characters' moral dilemmas, where multiple emotions and motives collide within her characters. As they make their way through a compelling story full of self-reflection and contemplation about the complex, tangled web of emotions they feel, the characters are forced to confront their own moral compass and the societal norms that shape their actions.

Christie's stories delve into the lives of characters who, like the readers, wrestle with moral issues, face themselves, and change continuously. These delicate inner journeys of the human soul integrated into Christie's stories reflect more than the fictional world of entertainment and provide helpful explanations for the balance of good and evil in human life. Through the myriad characters in Christie's world, it is Christie's world that readers undergo a metamorphosis, comprehending the multifaceted nature of good and evil that simply cannot be reduced to binary opposition.

The Impact of the Environment on Human Behaviour

Different surroundings influence mankind's actions and tendencies, and Agatha Christie intimately understood this balance showcased through her writing. From the peaceful English villages to the lavish grand estates, Christie brilliantly utilises the psychological impact of a setting's environment on character behaviour. In each of her tales, the setting operates as a powerful actor that determines the behaviour and intentions of people. Every location, whether the lonesome island from 'And Then There Were None' or the busy train ride in 'Murder on the Orient Express', is a central character alongside the web of human behaviour.

Moreover, Christie intricately entwines social standards, interpersonal relationships, and historical contexts into settings that significantly shape the human mind. The sociological differences between towns and cities, the impact of social stratification, and the place and manner it was set are essential in constructing a character. By interrelating all of these, Christie dives deep within the waters of humanity, illustrating that man is highly influenced by the context and environment around him or her.

Furthermore, her stories' vivid descriptions transport readers to different places and times while simultaneously revealing moral complexities laden with psychological conflict.

The dreadful tone in landscape and architecture elicits profound discomfort, which highlights the effects one's environment has on the mind. In her novels, Christie vividly describes setting with the intent to make readers consider the impact beyond factors of morality, ethics, norms, and irrational reasoning on conduct.

Within this context, we perceive Christie's exceptional literary talents. Every one of her settings is crafted with rich detail that goes beyond serving merely as a backdrop for her moving stories; they serve to actively shape the psychology of the people who inhabit them. Readers traverse through richly developed settings, forcing them to understand humanity's intricate nature and how people and places are interdependent. Her mastery of weaving diverse environments and exploring their relationship dynamics continues to delight audiences and define and affirm Christie's status as a master of sophisticated literature that incorporates sophisticated psychology and vice versa.

Conclusion: The Evolution of Intricacy

Revisiting Agatha Christie's timeless literature makes it easy to appreciate her sophisticated understanding of human behaviour and relationships. Christie drew her inspiration from the art of deception and created plots infused with complex character construction, social interaction, and psychological intricacies. Beyond the bounds of detective fiction, Christie's work is an intricate puzzle of the evolving human psyche, showcasing her ability to paint lifelike multi-dimensional mysteries.

Christie's journey as a developing author makes it easier to see her incorporation of complexity and detail, polishing her earlier work and ultimately leading to greater mastery in what would later become her renowned novels. Her earlier stories seemed simpler, revolving around riddled plot sequences wrapped in clever deceit. As time passed, Christie began offering deeper insight into morality and exceeded expectations through her ethical quandaries combined with complex motives and actions. The beauty in her surreal stories lies in their transcendence across time and era and their ability to reflect timeless concepts of humanity, regardless of genre.

In retrospect, Christie's sharp understanding of intricacy goes beyond the details and extends to the potential of her work as a whole, seeing beyond themes and characters showcased individually.

It includes the shifting societal framework in which her stories were set. The evolution of forensic science and criminology, the construction of gender and social norms in society, and the portrayal of gender and social norms are all balanced for intricate gender dynamics. Her mastery as a storyteller involuntarily shapes the life experiences of people with which her readers are likely to relate closely.

Her storytelling makes it clear that in addition to Agatha Christie being a skilful master of disguised integrations, she is unquestionably intelligent enough to apply diverse layers of understanding of human emotions, psychologically and sociologically, by creating elaborate fantasies. Regardless of boundaries placed by classic crime literature, Agatha's texts tend to unlock new dimensions along with countless dimensions of study, making her work endlessly appealing. Gradually, as we dive deeper into the shift and Christie's intricacies, we slowly observe the nuances embedded in the story and find answers to timeless questions.

5

Poirot, Marple, and Iconic Characters

Building Legends

Origins and Inspirations: Crafting Timeless Detectives

The origins of Agatha Christie's detectives can be considered timeless, as they reveal the rich tapestry of influences that informed the works of her detectives. Christie's interest in psychology and crime-solving began in her formative years when she keenly observed sophisticated social dissection, which informed her behaviour and later became foundational to her narratives. As a pharmacy dispenser during WWI, she gained a wealth of experience with poisons and medicines that intricately found their way into her narratives involving murders and mysterious deaths. Furthermore, her travels with her second husband, Max Mallowan, to archaeological sites in the Middle East exposed her not only to a myriad of cultures and customs but also allowed her to enrich the narrative of international intrigue embedded in her stories.

Also, the impact of her girlhood in Torquay, with its charming topography and sociable people, provided her with valuable insight into the nature of people, which she used to develop the various intricate characters she created. From these distinctive cultures, Christie created Hercule Poirot and Miss Marple. She gave them unique personalities, quirks, and ways of solving mysteries that still appeal to readers and audiences across the globe. Christie's fascination with order, precision, and intellect is seen in the fastidious Belgian detective Poirot, who showcased these traits alongside an unparalleled understanding of human nature. In contrast, Christie's belief in the power of quiet observation and the underestimated wisdom of elderly women is showcased in Miss Marple, who, with her meek demeanour, reveals an uncommon understanding of human behaviour.

Agatha Christie's characters were not just products of her imagination, but also reflections of the society she deeply observed. Her narratives were enriched by the intricate psychological details she had gathered from a lifetime of immersive study. The timeless detectives she created, such as Hercule

Poirot and Miss Marple, continue to capture the attention of people around the globe, a testament to the fusion of precise historical context, personal experiences, and a deep understanding of human nature that Christie brought to her writing.

Hercule Poirot: The Conception of a Methodical Mind

Agatha Christie's sterling creation, Hercule Poirot, is second to none in Christie's world. The blend of a disciplined mind with a keen eye for detail gives birth to Poirot, who is self-sufficient in booking passage on any ship that sails Filipino waters! Throughout Poirot's several adventures, Christie meticulously reflects on her approach towards plot construction, which requires sharp sleuthing and attention to detail. For the consumption of the French image, the character was carved out of Christie's experiences during work at a dispensary, mingling with Belgian refugees towards the end of the Great War. As enigmatic as Christie's evolving writing skills were, so was Poirot, who, over the years, underwent extensive character development accompanying the societal changes across the globe.

A Belgian who gained fame as one of the most stylish characters in detective fiction was journeying through England, where he managed to create an ensemble of bras and girdles in his imagination. Stylish to the core, Poirot, with his fastidious mannerisms, managed to blend into society with relative ease.

The explosion of the Covid-19 pandemic boosted construction works in England, leading to streets filled with structural wonders. Parallel, streets resonated with the thoughts of old, frail people, abstaining from going outside on a hot summer day, all set to blend into England's newest fascination, industrial strikes, while the borders remained shut.

After his first debut in 'The Mysterious Affair at Styles,' there was no looking back for Poirot. Throughout Christie's novels, she sowed fragments of reality within her fiction, captivating the hearts of readers around the globe.

Poirot's unique mannerisms and sharp mind flawlessly combine with the story's plot structure, embedding themselves within the walls of timeless literature. Moreover, his influence cuts way deeper than the written word since his character has been adapted for stage and screen, affirming his legendary status in crime fiction. The embrace of his character in various forms enables him to amass newer fans while fortifying his position among seasoned followers. In creating Hercule Poirot, Christie enhanced the art of detective fiction and exposed us to the struggles of humanity, forever changing the world of literature.

Miss Marple: The Gentle Yet Shrewd Observer

With Miss Jane Marple, an endless Agatha Christie creation, we appreciate the author's ability to capture the spirit of the crafty gentlewoman. Miss Marple lives in the peaceful small village of St. Mary Mead, where she takes an active interest in people, unravelling difficult situations using her keen intuition and psychological insight. She, unlike Poirot, uses knowledge of people and situations instead of abstraction and deduction. This makes her character rather different in the world of detective stories. Miss Marple's passion towards the everyday deceptions and crimes in the lives of mundane people leads us to understand that she's a character rooted within existence rather than above it. As such, readers attain an interesting glimpse into deeply rooted human nature and issues beneath everyday life's surface. The puzzle of finding and exposing a culprit is made whole by Marple meeting different types of people. Through these interactions, Christie works with and within social relations, roles of people, and relations in henpecked widows' manners and comes out with charming realism. It is sufficient to say that Christie incorporated rich reality with her imagination because she gave exceptional attention to the personalities, prose, and other characters meeting Miss Marple.

Her unswerving attention to detail in each case demonstrates the resolve and determination that is synonymous with Miss Marple's character. It will be noted, for example, that Christie's tension-laden yet charming style while depicting Miss Marple's affairs is delightful and remains ever-appealing. Truly, this combination of warmth, wisdom, and quiet strength makes Miss Marple one of the most beloved and enduring characters in literature. Miss Marple's enduring appeal transcends time, making her a character that continues to resonate with readers today.

Supporting Ensemble: Memorable Allies and Adversaries

In Agatha Christie's detailed stories, the protagonists and their supporting casts are depicted in a varied and rich manner. Whether it is the teenage crush who followed his favourite detective or the hated but similarly talented detective who vowed revenge on him, each adds a distinctive life to every mystery in Christie's works. Hercule Poirot and Miss Marple may take the stage, but they are supported by a myriad of unforgettable people who, in memorable ways, enhance the true richness and complexity of their adventures.

It is impossible to talk about Poirot without touching on his trusted friend and associate, Captain Arthur Hastings. Hastings not only serves as Poirot's aide-de-camp but also functions as his biographer, which means he respects and sometimes challenges Poirot's balancing of Poirot's mental marvels with steady scrutiny. Similarly, Ariadne Oliver, an eccentric portrayal of Christie herself, helps solve Poirot's cases using features unique to her personality.

Miss Marple has different supporting characters in her world, each of whom helps her intuitive nature expose deception and calumny. From the ever-vigilant companion Mr. Rafiel to the seemingly harmless villagers of St. Mary Mead, every person greatly helps Miss Marple make accurate deductions.

Apart from these aides, Christie's clever protagonists must face reckless villains. Dr. Sheppard is known for being unreachable, a claim he fiercely defends in "The Murder of Roger Ackroyd." Colonel Race, who is featured in several novels, is also a great example. Always ready to plot against Christie's protagonists, these characters infuriate Poirot and Marple while capturing the readers with their unparalleled wit. Bouquets of logic and crafts of cunning alter every narrative crafted by Christie's redoubt.

A character or two might provide indispensable aid, while others sprinkle just the right seeds of distrust and different complexities in Christie's carefully crafted intricacies. As Christie spins this tale of friends and foes, readers get hooked on a story world where every character more than just fulfils a role in solving the enigma presented, regardless of how little their part is. From the blend of these divergent personalities, Christie gives us an immortal experience, a masterpiece capturing human motivations and behaviour.

Character Evolution: Growth Across the Canon

The evolution of characters is intrinsically linked to Agatha Christie, exhibiting the great detail and polish she added to her characters' personas. Across her canon, readers naturally observe the characters' evolution, offering insight into exploring human nature and development. From Hercule Poirot's refinement to Miss Marple's witticism, Christie immerses her characters and audience in a series of events and struggles that guide them to adapt and showcase remarkable resilience. This evolution goes beyond single narratives and invites readers to invest completely in the characters' progression. Moreover, Poirot's early cases and chronicles show exponential insight and emotional depth growth. At the same time, Miss Marple illustrates the gradual development of human behaviour comprehension, showing evolution in society's understanding. The recurring characters' growing complexity and internal tensions testify to Christie's incredible storytelling skills, transforming her characters from mere caricatures into complex entities that undergo ceaseless changes. Exposing layers of their psyche, Christie's portrayal of evolving characters within the boundaries of crime fiction archetypes transcends typical character expectations, surpassing the bounds of fiction as multidimensional beings crafted with emotional arcs.

Furthermore, the interdependence of character development and plot structure has a distinct effect on the narrative by adding another layer of depth to every story, which enables readers to connect with it on a completely different level. Throughout the canon, Christie traces the development of her characters and, in doing so, bestows upon them timeless lessons, reflecting the change and growth that is inherent in humanity. Her imaginative realms serve as backdrops to enthralling mysteries, yet her characters transcend entertainment; they invite profound contemplation about change and self within vibrant landscapes. The attention to minute details and thorough consideration of the characters' arcs establishes

Christie as a master of literature's foundational pillars. Her characters and their transformations, which remain relevant across generations, enrich literature with profound representations of the evolution of humanity, illustrating her remarkable skill in crafting compelling narratives.

Literary Techniques: Building Depth through Dialogue and Description

In Agatha Christie's complex world of literary works, mastery of detail construction through dialogue serves to capture readers' attention. Characters emerge from their shells, revealing diverse and complex personalities, motives, and bonds that drive the plot. Every revelation, every twist and turn owes a great deal to Christie's choice of dialogue. Christie has skillfully constructed her dialogues filled with great red herrings, subtle clues, and revelations, aiding the readers' understanding of her diverse characters. The portrayal of the witty exchanges between Hercule Poirot and his friends showcases the brilliant mastery of language, revealing nuances that add rich complexity to the dynamics of the investigation. Also, the astute dialogue illuminating Miss Marple's observations and her ability to deduce reason and logic grants profound insight into human and societal behaviour. Apart from dialogue, descriptions done by Christie serve best in the vividly crafted English countryside and the exotic locations where her tales shuttle the readers. Every detail provided is intricately woven into the works, enveloping readers in the English dawn's grandeur ethos.

The narrations come to life with vivid imagery and sensory details, placing readers in an immersive visual and emotional experience. The way Christie blends dialogue and description demonstrates her multi-faceted literary skill by constructing a narrative that profoundly affects audiences. She remarkably intertwines plot progression and character development with the background context of society using well-crafted literary techniques, resulting in profound immersion in her stories. This captivating fusion of dialogue and description enchants readers beyond time and culture, solidifying Christie's enduring legacy in mystery and detective fiction.

Culture Reflection: Societal Impact Through Her Characters

Christie's works have a profound cultural impact, largely due to characters like Hercule Poirot and Miss Marple. With their unique traits, these characters captivate the audience and contribute to developing cultural attitudes and practices. They are not just reflections of the societies they inhabit but also evoke the experiences and emotions of the people. Through their character traits and behaviours, Christie's characters address many social challenges, ethical issues, and the class strife of her time, which persists into the present day.

Issues of justice, morality, the human condition, and the

undercurrents between the lines highlighting social relations receive attention through the clever detection of Hercule Poirot and his characters. The meticulous nature of the character and his strong sense of right and wrong serve both consumption and greater societal matters—truth and the obscured ethical motives that lurk in human actions. Together with Miss Marple, her remarkable insights into human nature enable the comprehension of gerontological and power structures of gender discrimination and community dominion.

Christie's loyal and attentive sidekicks, as well as her witty antagonists, serve to reflect more profoundly on social relations concerning ethnic diversity. They are epitomes of social conflict and contact from civilised society. They reflect emerging sociological issues related to understanding middle-class prejudices, misconceptions, empathy, and social solidarity and ignore the social barrier divide. Christie's characters are not just tools for advancing the plot but deeply developed individuals who reflect the complexities of society and human nature.

Agatha Christie created her characters to engage with the world as it is and address sensitive issues and social taboos through mystery. Their timeless relevance speaks volumes about the author's insight into human nature and her ability to weave ethical and philosophical questions into her works. Furthermore, the enduring popularity of these characters across various adaptations, including stage and television, is a testament to their continuing significance and impact on culture. This enduring relevance ensures that readers, regardless of their background or time period, can connect with and be engaged by Christie's works.

The Interplay of Plot and Personality: Crafted Crime Logic

Like the rest of her works, Agatha Christie was and is best known for her novels' interplay of plot and personality. Christie's character development and plot construction sophistication go hand in hand due to the dense canvas of their character attributes with which she metaphorically paints her stories. The marriage between the advancement of the events of a story and character sketching in a novel, or vice versa, is something she has mastered throughout her life. Engrossed in the whirlpool of mysteries, the readers are frequently fascinated with the effortless melting of these components marvellously integrated into every unique mystery linked with individual character development. Christie's sophisticated virtuosity is perhaps most prominent in developing her characters, whom she provides with motives and complexities intertwined with the story's events. Each quirk, every description, and every tale set forth serves two equally important functions: to advance the story in a reasonable direction and to project the sociological aspect of her narratives. How she way instructs the logic of her crime mysteries goes beyond the logic of puzzles, as it reaches the desperate depths for the living reasons behind the acts of the crime criminal and the investigator's activated from careful observation and skilful use of misleading clues redirection allows Christie to expertly guide her readers through complex narratives while simultaneously offering thrill. The characters' personal flaws and intricate backgrounds also add texture that fuels the appeal's depth and heightens the mystery's stakes. The mystery deepens as Christie's balance of character psychology and sophisticated plot intricacies entices the readers to participate mentally and emotionally. The solution is no longer an unveiling of the perpetrator but an exposition of the inherent human condition in all of its vulnerabilities and complexities. This interdependence solidifies Christie's impact on the crime fiction genre while simultaneously marking her charm to remain forever in history.

Reader Enchantment: Cultivating Curiosity and Engagement

The fascination surrounding Agatha Christie's crimes is intricately plotted and meticulously sleuthed. Her equally captivating talent prepares readers' senses of curiosity and engagement while keeping them on the edge of their seats. Christie intricately blends nuances of human nature, society, art, and deductions into riveting tales of intrigue. Christie's immersion skills compel her readers to solve the mysteries of the great detectives because of her remarkable characters and attention to detail. She truly has a gift in making people want to take part in solving the mysteries.

Christie's reader enchantment stems from the skilful balance of revelation and concealment of information. With carefully placed clues and red herrings, she leads her audience through bewilderment and deduction. The lack of resolution enhances the challenge she presents through unrelenting plots but also tends to require a great deal of page-turning attention to solve the mystery. Every mystery is designed to drag the reader into the whirlpool and make them feel part of the grand scheme while untangling countless deceptive strings.

Furthermore, Christie's prose possesses an effortless appeal which is universal in scope, resonating with people everywhere. Her skilful writing creates wonder and delight, encouraging readers to explore the imagination that comes with her richly crafted worlds. Whether in exotic settings or quaint English villages, Christie's storytelling never fails to bring the reader to the very centre of the mystery, powerfully capturing the reader's imagination and ensuring lasting emotional engagement with the text.

In addition, the enchantment brought to readers by the depth and development of Christie's beloved recurring characters like Hercule Poirot and Miss Marple is remarkable. These familiar faces, quirky as they might be, are bound to win the loyalty of the readers who wait impatiently for the next revelation. Through unique quirks and age-old wisdom, these detectives become favourite book characters and captivate readers because of their remarkable intelligence.

At its core, the ingenuity of Agatha Christie's work can be appreciated in the effective blending of complex plots, rich text, and striking characterisation as they work toward one singular goal: invoking curiosity and engaging the audience. All the elements create a world that resonates with the readers and deeply intertwines their heartstrings with the mysteries that unfold in front of them. This ability to enthral readers across age gaps has established her as the only Queen of Crime and a timeless literature icon.

Legacy of Legends: Enduring Popularity in Modern Media

As Agatha Christie's stunning works constantly get new adaptations, her characters range from timeless classics to modern wonders. Hercule Poirot, Miss Marple, and other characters have existed across multiple generations, appealing to people far and wide. Their existence today makes more sense than ever as they exist in films, television shows, and even video games. With captivating storytelling and brilliant adaptations, such characters thrive in the modern era. The phenomenal attention to detail that was the hallmark of Christie's pieces is now even more significant in adaptations, enhancing her cinematic and televisual portrayal in a way that does justice and brings her original vision to life. The careful detail forming poisons legacy is a testament to Christie's brilliance. The multifaceted and ever-evolving portrayal of Agatha Christie's characters is a significant pillar in attracting interest in these works. Hercule Poirot's unmatched ingenuity leaves people spellbound as they indulge in a world of ever-present embellishments of his persona while also being captivated by his outstanding intellect. Furthermore, Miss Marple exemplifies a blend of unassuming but perceptive, which helps audiences connect to the characters deeper, making them relatable but formidable.

Additionally, the mysteries encompassing these characters can make them malleable to many forms of storytelling that different audiences might appreciate. This flexibility has permitted new-age storytellers to develop new ideas while still preserving the core spirit of these characters deeply loved by audiences everywhere, broadening their charm and influence. Also, the enduring presence of these characters in contemporary media is further evidence of Christie's enduring insight into humanity and the popularity of a well-written detective novel. The unresolved issues in her stories—lies, human behaviour, ethical dilemmas, and justice—are just as important today as they were when these iconic characters were first brought to life. Modern adaptations have succeeded in connecting with devoted supporters and new consumers by using Christie's cherished characters and turning them into modern-day tales, bringing Christie's characters further into the spotlight. As society moves further into digital technology, we can be sure that the fascination with Hercule Poirot, Miss Marple, and other timeless icons will endure and adapt to different forms of modern media, captivating generations to come through ongoing evolution.

6

The War's Influence

Nursing, Pharmacy, and Tragedy

Beginning for the Effects of the War on Literature

Literature worldwide has evolved over centuries due to different conflicts and their ways of being expressed. In the fundamental structure, literature has always tried to capture the essence of everything that defines humanity, including its violence. It draws upon our primaeval spirit, bringing forth artistry steeped in our profound realities. As the climate metamorphosises with the ever-growing tempests of War, writers are gripped such that they cannot help but witness the anatomy of unrivalled power/Violence, morality, and Absurdism woven through existence. This part describes hyperbolic tales of violence and the achievements of creativity that stemmed from the gruesome experience of war/violence. The greatness brought forth by Agatha Christie is a fine thread with which we may weave an even greater tale in understanding how Literature has written back to Warfare not only in words but remnants infused with Trauma and memories that time cannot erode.

Engaging with this genre of literature reveals the intricate blend of suffering, strength, and ethical frameworks that persist in our psyche, showcasing yet again the enduring impact of war on writing throughout history.

The Call to Service: Christie as a Volunteer Nurse

As the world was engulfed in the fire of World War I, Agatha Christie bravely answered her country's call by working as a volunteer nurse. Her experiences in the frontline hospitals, witnessing the immense physical and psychological trauma of war, must have profoundly changed her approach to writing. Her deep commitment to her role as a nurse, coupled with the stark realities of wartime healthcare, undoubtedly left an indelible mark on her future books. Her myriad of interactions with the war patients enabled her to experience human suffering and conflict on a level which she later artistically employed in her masterpieces.

Christie's experience as a volunteer nurse also altered her

understanding of proper medical practices and procedures, which aided in the authenticity of her fiction. Working with the wounded developed Christie's empathy and sharpened her observational skills, allowing her to perceive even the faintest details of mankind and life itself.

Christie's profound experiences as a volunteer nurse during the war not only deepened the level of emotion and empathy in her stories but also transformed her literary capabilities. Her work during the conflict, especially, shaped her understanding of selflessness and sacrifice, enriching her craft with unparalleled authenticity. The war was a crucible that honed her skills, allowing her to craft compelling characters and plots that resonate with readers to this day.

Christie certainly understood the unrelenting nature of war and its impact on an individual on a deeper level. Witnessing the sheer strength and fragility war inflicted, paired with her strong understanding of vulnerability, fuelled her literary voice. With her artistic lens, she captured the trauma and tender spirit of resilience, breaking new boundaries in fortifying the human spirit and exploring them throughout her writings. These insights must have greatly impacted her life, crafting the profound lens through which she could shape compelling characters and plots.

Medicinal Insights: The Role of Pharmacy in Plot Development

As a famous writer who enjoyed crafting complex plots and paying attention to details, Agatha Christie's embrace of pharmacy as a literary device is undoubtedly one of her many captivating traits. Christie incorporates pharmacy knowledge into her mysteries to an astounding degree and remarkably integrates pharmaceutical information into her mysteries, which she undoubtedly gained from her time as a volunteer nurse. The way she uses medications, their effects, and the potential abuse of character motivations and actions is deeply nuanced.

One of the most dramatic recurring devices in her works, perhaps taken too lightly, is that of poisoning. Christie's ability to illustrate the potency of many dangerous substances showcases her mastery of pharmaceutical sciences. In Christie's works, whether administering deadly quantities or the clever subtlety of poisoning seemingly innocent mixtures, the use of pharmacy in her works serves a greater purpose; it unveils the complexities of mankind.

Moreover, the inclusion of pharmaceutical details makes her stories more believable. Christie enthrals readers by binding them to the world through its verisimilitude in her narratives. In particular, her drug interactions, dosages, and access control of these substances add to the realism of her novels.

It is noted that Christie's pharmacy skills blend into her plots, focusing on trust and betrayal, which is deeply emphasised throughout her novels. The deceitful nature dominating her narratives is sharply exposed through the manipulation of medications and poisons. These ruthless protagonists who use pharmaceutical skills for their unscrupulous goals embody the complex sinister deception within humans.

Christie's pharmacy knowledge, elaborated upon in her stories, displays her creativity in dealing with plots, making them even more interesting. Her consideration of medicinal elements within her stories demonstrates her mastery and ability to construct captivating narratives, which have continued to be appreciated over the years, proving her skill as the Queen of Crime.

War-Time Realities: How Conflict Shaped Storytelling

The impact of the conflict was evident in the life works of Agatha Christie and numerous others during the World War I period. It served as a conflict-driven point that boosted writing into new dimensions. Agatha and many others explored their creativity during the global conflict and used it as inspiration for books and writings. Not only did authors find new plots, but they also explored severely tested human endurance and nature. The war provided a unique backdrop for storytelling, allowing authors to delve into the depths of human experience and resilience in the face of adversity.

Along with other thriving novelists, Agatha and Christie drifted away from romance books full of bouts and inspiration. After witnessing gruesome fighting, they used the period of chaos to depict raw human nature and its mental landscape. They narrated the reality of war, which was emotionally sight-shattering. A new sense of realism overtook fiction, with countless writers striving to define the human condition in violence.

Those who survived such gruesome periods were engulfed in agony, which pushed them into melancholy. The new authors, along with Agatha, twisted these portrayals into mysteries, full of sorrow, where the characters struggled with endless grief in their personal alien wars. The captivating character development in these works led people to reflect.

As previously noted, the conflict of war profoundly impacted their multidimensional character portrayal. Protagonists were no longer basic caricatures, one-dimensional heroes; they were instead deeper reflections of people placed in complex and extraordinary situations and needed to reflect the far more nuanced truths of the world. This shift provided ample room for further examination of morality, choice, sacrifice, and the human ability to have hope, even when surrounded by hopelessness and despair.

With the change of societal conflict came the fundamental restructures of storytelling, used as a coping mechanism to make sense of the world's unprecedented changes. Storytelling allowed readers to witness the shocks and griefs of the war that had ravaged their world. This was the case for Christie and many other authors who profoundly restructured the evolving human condition using the power of storytelling and caused an irreparable shift in the literary world in a bid to showcase humanity's suffering.

The mark of storytelling met its undying imprint during the war, not exclusively to highlight its historical context. Around this period, literature was elevated to delve into the many introspective nature through profound shifts. Differentiating the essence of suffering, at the core of human resilience and vulnerability, authors managed to navigate the challenges of personal growth in chaos, resulting in storytelling that transformed once and for all, and continues to inspire future readers to this day.

Catalyst For Change: Personal Growth Amid Chaos

The still-raging World War II profoundly changed Agatha Christie's life, spending her entire childhood during the Blitz. During this period, full of troubles and problems, the writer faced new challenges, such as refreshing old ideas to improve her craft and develop as a new creator. Her learning curve required tackling harsh challenges to carve out the upcoming path. The war radically changed her perception of the world and made her confront how human life can be so easily fragile. She started to better understand palpable themes filled with a horrifying atmosphere that her life struggles created.

On top of that, all war necessities that broke requirements led Christie to explore beyond a new geography filled with grief, love, and strength. During this transformational phase, the writer began developing many new works, focusing on cultivating an understanding of the feelings experienced by universal people suffering during this period. In the middle of conflict, both actual and modern to her life, this experience has decreased her sensitivity but increased her value to other headlines or writers.

Her experiences with tragedy and loss gave her a deep understanding of the human spirit, enhancing her storytelling in a way that was more than just fiction. Her writing reflected the unyielding human spirit that survives in difficult times, capturing her growth experience amidst turmoil. For Christie, the chaotic setting of war served as both the catalyst and muse for her exploration of the depths of human nature, inspiring a timeless legacy.

Tragedies Unveiled: Loss and Transformation in Christie's Life

Agatha Christie's life took a tragic turn right when she began her career as a writer. The most noteworthy event was the disappearance of Archie Christie, her first husband, in 1926. Archie's disappearance resulted in a media frenzy that took a toll on both her personal life and her career in literature.

In one form or another, the two world wars had Agatha exposed to brutal suffering. During the First World War, Agatha volunteered as a nurse, which further opened her eyes to the horrors of war. Their experiences of the war and her losses heavily influenced the way she wrote, portraying feelings of profound loss, trauma and suffering. Her mother's death and her first marriage collapse led to an initial period of upheaval in her life. Those profound emotional upheavals, combined with the societal changes and the currents of complex history, changed Christie herself. This change looks euphorically through her novels' perfectly woven layers of emotions and psychological insight.

Even with the challenges, Christie's ability to remain self-reflective is evident as she confronts the grief-stricken metamorphosis. How she turned heart-wrenching grief into fascinating stories filled those narratives with depth. Such stories are relatable even as the world advances. The vulnerability of humankind aids in shaping, "infuses" seems to permeate the characters and plots of her novels, making her timeless.

Sketching the fragments of her life reveals a spectrum of emotions, including intense despair intertwined with hope and perseverance. She expressed the intricate balancing act of confronting loss and summoning strength while traversing Christie's journey toward healing through the art of literature. Her struggles were transcended into incredible writing pieces, proving the impact of creativity and the boundless imagination of Christie's life.

Character Development: War-Time Archetypes in Her Work

The backdrops of the two terrible World Wars profoundly

affected Agatha Christie's literary works and greatly influenced her characters' development. While people coped with the chaos caused by the wars, Christie provided insight into war-life archetypes and gave life to centuries of experiences through her skilful storytelling.

In Christie's work, a great conflict embodies wartime archetypes as morally perplexed, multi-dimensional characters, showcasing the high human price of the war. The intertwining suffering of a war and identity crisis is strongly felt in these characterisations of a hero turned anti-hero and a selfless character drowned in utter moral chaos.

Additionally, the shifting gender relations and roles during the war years incorporate themselves into Christie's characterisations, such as the working women who emerge as the new, adaptive heroines of a changing world. These portrayals mark the change of attitudes in society and the struggle of women forced into different roles due to the absence of men.

Furthermore, Christie's work also notes the figure of the soldier, especially the soldier who has to deal with life after enduring the challenges of war, a recurring theme in post-war literature. This highlights the clearly observable post-war disillusionment and the psychological consequences of the war on its survivors. Christie explores the minds of these characters and provides commentary on the emotional and mental consequences of war.

Trust, betrayal, relationships, balance, and conflict are interlinked in Christie's wartime archetypes, where she seeks to define human relations. This serves as a reminder of the alienation that individuals became prey to in wartime society and showcases the erosion of trust and uncertainty as the dominating feelings amplified by war.

In one way or another, Christie's deft characterisation of wartime archetypes surely showcases her depth of understanding of people during harrowing times of war. Throughout her works, the war-induced struggles of Christie's characters highlight her perception of battle's effect on humanity; her wit and literary mastery capture the reader's attention, showcasing the devastating consequences of conflict while simultaneously celebrating the spirit of hope.

Authenticity Through Experience: Bridging Fiction and Reality

After the war, Agatha Christie's exploration of nursing and pharmacy deepened her understanding and empathy and proved a valuable fountain of nursing and fiction material. Her work as a volunteer nurse during the First World War engendered a deep connection with suffering and psychosocial resilience, infusing her writing with real emotions and psychological understanding. In bridging the gulf between the stark reality of war and the fictional world, Christie seamlessly merged these two worlds. With her experiences and observations, she was able to portray her characters and stories with a sense of genuineness that reflected the human spirit even in trying times. The trauma and turmoil of war firsthand experienced by Christie enabled her to understand the intricate nature of a human being, which helped her create rich, multi-dimensional characters that resonated with readers deeply.

Furthermore, her job in the pharmacy exposed her to the intricacies of practices, which she expertly wove into the storylines of her works. This gave her narratives added depth and realism. Merging real-life elements with Christie's aptitude for fiction is one of the trademarks of her captivating works, which garnered global attention. Due to Christie's wartime influences, her stories attain remarkable civilisation-level realism in detail, and her portrayal of the human condition is made possible. As such, Christie's lived experiences and her ability to capture human behaviour set her as a transcendental fiction-reality master storyteller.

Post-War Reflections: Adapting Themes for a New Era

Having experienced the reality of a world at war, Agatha Christie found herself at the peak of societal change alongside cultural transformation. The war deeply impacted her personal life and literary traits. Changes in her writing style during the post-war era showcased evolving themes and characters, providing a unique historical connection for readers.

Christie's stories began to illustrate the hope and resilience throughout the conflicts that shaped the world during the war-torn periods of her life. Her narratives were filled with themes of reparation, justice, and the complex sides of human nature, which mirrored society's desperate desire to heal. Christie's characters underwent a significant shift; those who struggled with the war's consequences had to transition into more profound and vulnerable figures to showcase the pre-and post-war mentality.

The author's profound understanding of societal change during and after the war aligned perfectly with the intricacies of her detective fiction. This post-war period served as a new era for her to analyse the new shifting patterns regarding power, loyalty, and trust. The gradual change in interactions among her fictional characters served as an intricate portrayal of a society fighting to reconstruct its imagery while dealing with rebuilding human relationships.

Alongside that, Christie's deep understanding of the psychological impact of war enhanced the depth of her writings. She skillfully crafted stories that showcase human determination while revealing the hidden frailty that accompanied it. Her narratives adopted a profound perspective, dealing with the loss of innocence and the desperate attempt to build a foundation in a new reality.

Also, female protagonists in her novels changed profoundly with significant modernisation, unlike in earlier novels that exhibit the late Christie period in correspondence with the role women were expected to play in post-war society. These women were strong and resilient individuals who sought complete independence. This demonstrated the slow societal adaptation towards encroaching the 21st century and enabling the transformation considering women's rights.

When Christie's works developed towards the post-war period, they completely integrated her experience of storytelling that spanned across different periods in time. She was capable of generating poignant narratives with a sense of new beginnings and self-reflection and guiding readers into understanding the inner adaptive nature of the human spirit. Therefore, the post-war undertones of Christie's fiction works indicate her remarkable reputation as the Queen of Crime and in the study of sociology.

Conclusion and Transition: From Turmoil to Inspiration

As we reach the final chapter of our review of Agatha Christie's life and works, it is notable how her experiences in the pre-war and post-war periods almost seamlessly fit her storytelling. The chaotic war events during Christie's lifetime significantly changed her psyche, transforming her writing style and predominant themes. However, she was not only affected negatively. The chaos surrounding pleading and suffering strife drew a deep well of creative inspiration for Christie as she expressed harnessing the pain and complexities of human emotions and behaviour during troubling times.

For Christie, an enabling post-war world alongside her sharpened pen brought forth a marked turning point in her career. This was the era she balanced, bearing witness to the destruction while stepping into a landscape overflowing with opportunities. The characters in her writings also underwent similar transformative changes, revealing hopes and dreams towards the shifting societal dynamics. The imagination of Christie's sharp observing eyes gave birth to the stories that once captivatingly told the tale and now stand as a reflection of their time.

Her works after the war prominently showcased resilience, inner strength, and the human spirit. Agatha Christie's storytelling was unique in that she skillfully constructed elaborate plots containing pieces concerning the nature of humans. The cleansing fires of conflict did inspire turbulence, but it relinquished its grip upon the literary world and marked its nature for eternity in Christie's stories.

In summary, Christie's life, which passed from the shadows of war into an illuminating period, embodies a vivid expression of creativity and imagination, enduring alongside her stories for years to come. In her literature, Christie does not merely entertain; she delivers deep and sincere messages of compassion and empathy. Transitioning from the radiance of an imagined world to the tragedies of war speaks volumes of Christie's brilliance and sensitivity towards the complexities of human life.

Emerging from the conflict, Christie gained new insight and wisdom. This newfound perception led her to inspire future generations with her ageless stories. Agatha's legacy has become a reminder that from mankind's dark periods, hope will always arise through storytelling.

7

Exotic Inspirations

Travels with Max Mallowan

The Mallowan Expeditions

The reasoning behind Agatha Christie and Max Mallowan's expeditions throughout the Middle East was deeply influenced by their sense of adventure, which in turn greatly impacted their personal and professional lives. The region's captivating exotic sites, ancient history, and rich culture were incredibly important to Christie's literary works, inspiring her stories with an authentic sense of time and place. This also greatly benefited Mallowan, as his archaeological pursuits offered plenty of reasons for her travels, considering he conducted numerous excavations and research projects in cooperation with local experts. Their shared passion for adventure drove them to the remote regions of the Middle East, which turned out to be an inspiring treasure trove for Christie's gripping narratives. It is also worth noting that the couple's respect for the customs they encountered fostered a profound appreciation towards the essence of human history and storytelling, along with the incredible diversity that each destination provided. Ultimately, the Mallowan expeditions are a primary example of the blend of intellectual curiosity, artistic inspiration, and cultural immersion - a spirit of exploration throughout all of Christie's literary works.

The Middle Eastern Sojourn: A New Source of Inspiration

The travels of Agatha Christie with Max Mallowan gave Christie a new impetus for her writing. The change was in the form of the Middle Eastern culture, which she had never experienced before. The Middle East provided Mallowan with numerous archaeological opportunities and fuelled Christie's desire to travel after the sojourn in England.

The mesmerising sites of archaeological construction enriched with ancient relics fuelled Christie's imagination and chronicled a magnificent region. The vibrant erstwhile civilisations that lie in shambles provided modules of fiction only waiting to be scripted. Spending time with Mallowan, Christie acquired a great understanding of the culture, which in turn infused her work with inspirations of vibrant life. This enabled her to develop prose that had a foundational factual essence and laid claim to truthful history.

The striking contrast between the blistering deserts and the graceful monuments shaped Christie's experience. In her mind, the rich charm of the traditional architecture mixed with the mystery of the winding bazaars as shadow and light danced over the dunes. Christie describes this very feeling when depicting the Middle East in her literature; indeed, the backdrop's vividness is always tangible in her works.

The region's captivating folklore also deeply enriched her understanding of the local culture. Through local customs and traditions, such as sharing traditional meals, Christie and Mallowan not only embraced the life of a local but also deeply respected and appreciated the culture, which transformed their outlook and Christie's writings. Their mastery of cultural understanding is showcased by the seamless blend of the culture diffused throughout her narratives, which gives them a unique sense of genuine beauty.

Fundamentally, the visit to the Middle East marked an important period in Agatha Christie's life. This is where the archaeological wonders, breathtaking scenery, and captivating blend of people and cultures met to form a new chapter in her work. It is evident that Christie's travels and experiences in the Middle East provided her with an abundant reservoir of inspiration, which made her storytelling unrivalled. She was able to infuse her works with a multicultural richness that rendered them beautiful and inspired countless readers.

Archaeological Insights: Dig Sites and Discoveries

Agatha Christie and her second husband, Maximilian 'Max' Mallowan, had intermingled personal interests, being deeply rooted in culture, travel, and archaeology. Christie's husband, Mallowan, was an archaeologist who led several excavations in the Middle East. With her unquenchable thirst for knowledge, Christie actively participated in his endeavours, gaining firsthand experience. Known to be an archaeology enthusiast, Christie utilised these excursions to gain inspiration for her work. During Mallowan's expeditions, the couple would marvel at ancient sites and civilisations, relishing their beauty. Christie's literary mind came to life as her inspiration for stories began with the excavations led by her husband and the sites Christie explored. Bound to Christie by the thrill of unearthing ancient artefacts, she experienced the archaeological expedition. As a result of Christie's immersion in the world of history, the excavation was the epiphany of her intellectual curiosity. United with compelling narratives, Christie was eagerly ready to document her experiences, and as she did during the process, her mind generated the most gripping stories.

Christie and the Desert Sun 'Beneath The Desert Sun, After Christie's Works' highlights her endless pursuits in archaeology that resulted in pristine, vivid narratives synchronised with her fiction concocted from fragments of her deep imagination. In doing so, Christie created powerful archaeological fiction with a strong sense of history. Her deep respect for the archaeologists whose work inspired her, alongside the work itself that generated profound reverence for previously buried worlds, led to Christie's scribbles burned into the pages of her history journal with an archaeological lens. After vivid imaginings and tales are told, an accurate mix of her thoughts and works enables readers to engage in intriguing stories with a depth far beyond fiction, taking them on a journey of adventure and endless treasure hunting while blending vibrant imaginations across time and eras.

Cultural Immersion: Embracing Local Customs

Unlike mere tourists, Agatha Christie and Max Mallowan participated in the culture while travelling through the Middle East. During their journeys, the couple sought to understand the people's way of life. From engaging in local ceremonies to interacting with local artisans, Christie and Mallowan did everything possible to learn about the various cultures and communities they encountered. Their meaningful, respectful curiosity enabled them to deeply understand different cultures and connected them in ways that later inspired Christie's perspectives on life and literature. This was only possible because Christie had developed a profound understanding of societal norms, rituals, and beliefs. In turn, this experience enriched her storytelling. Due to the deep understanding she gained by participating in local customs, she could weave spine-chilling realities throughout her novels that were relatable to readers around the globe. Apart from enhancing her worldview, the cultural experiences led her to appreciate the beauty inherent in diverse cultures, something she stunningly captures across her novels.

Christie's authentic representation of the places she visited has shaped the contours of literature and continues to influence literary audiences today. Her adoption of local customs fuelled her imaginative powers, allowing her to create rich narratives that guided readers to distant places steeped in culture and history.

Creative Exploration: Transforming Experiences into Narrative

From the markets to the vibrant bazaars, the sprawling ruins, and everything in between, Agatha Christie's experiences in the Middle Eastern region were augmented as she imagined new stories waiting to unfold in these corners of the world. She was a true traveller and an artist poised to absorb pieces of culture from every destination she immersed herself in. When she arrived, she didn't just visit. She absorbed these places and their localities, which later proved invaluable as the settings for her poignant stories, showered with detail and care.

When capturing realities and transforming them into experiences with zest, Christie's understanding of the imagination knew no bounds. Her keen nature made her travel reflective, allowing her to prevail outside the boundaries and naturally allure people to herself. She made cultures from around the world unite through the work she so gracefully chiselled while never leaving a grain of reality aside. The compassion for people bred away from home and the new faces she met during her travels allowed her realistic yet astonishing accounts to be repackaged into enchanting stories without being too outlandish.

The narrative carving was a labour of love for her, culminating in the gentle polishing of first impressions into crafted works. Every place was further enriched by its allure and beauty, which gave life to her imagination and was thus a rich source of her artistic endeavours. She turned the landscapes into mysteries, from gold covered in hills untold in Iraq to scenic, peaceful, sun-burnt calculus in Istanbul. She employed them in her books as literary gold. From the senses and feelings, the reader's presence was also given to description, but so was feeling for the culture surrounding her tale.

Also equally path-breaking is how she portrayed the different cultures and her take on social society dynamics: 'the locals' are so cleverly built into her plots of choice. It is clear that she expertly performed a balancing act between the cultural and social, and so her plot was enriched with intriguing and complex layers. Patchworks of imaginary components and reality showcased the essence captured through spirited journeys turned into multi-dimensional tales bursting with life. In addition to eluding bare entertainment, this easily flexible guide cleverly brought blockage in the form of borders to a reality beyond the boundaries we encounter every day, effortlessly shifting the exposed world we so eagerly wish to explore.

To sum up, Christie's imaginative investigation went beyond the limits of a plot's depiction to include sincere and profoundly moving recollections. A mark of Christie's creativity is her perspective of the world, which remains fascinating in all its variety, turning her literary works into everlasting treasures.

Characters with a Foreign Flair: Bringing Settings to Life

While Agatha Christie was travelling abroad with her husband Max Mallowan, she came across lavish cultures. The places a particular person travels to in their lifetime act as a source of inspiration. Agatha's varied cultural journeys are rich with memorable characters and themes which are beautifully woven into her stories.

When Christie travelled, there were people she encountered who had truly unique features. These features would shape their character in the most beautiful way, and Christie didn't waste any time putting these features to use. Trust me, every region has that one charming café owner and in this case it's a Turkish one. These characters were added to the already amazing structure of Christie's stories and made them remarkable.

Christie was keen to get to know the world around her. The people she met were profound and in-depth, and since she was a keen observer, along with a great storyteller, she crafted incredible tales without failing to maintain accuracy.

Her characters weren't superficial by any means. Instead, they stood tall as rich and complex individuals, ready to embark on that vivid journey crafted by Agatha herself.

Additionally, Christie's evocative treatment of her foreign setting's beauty demonstrates her sophisticated understanding and love of the world. Her detailed accounts and accurate representations of both the lively markets in Istanbul and Middle Eastern oases captured the imagination of readers, making them yearn for travel to these exotic places.

In addition, by merging her characters' stories with the development of her plots set in exotic locations, Christie shifted the boundaries of traditional storytelling into multidimensional, absorbing worlds filled with intricate narratives and sophisticated literature. Serving as both storytellers and guardians of these captivating realms, her characters represented the myriad cultures they came from, which made them relatable to the audience.

By incorporating characters of different nationalities into her books, Agatha Christie captured the richness of human cultures while showcasing the endless possibilities of storytelling and imagination, thus paving the way for future authors.

Collaboration and Companionship: Agatha and Max's Synergy

The relationship between Agatha Mallowan and archaeologist

Max Mallowan demonstrates how a marriage can be personal and professional. Max's firsthand understanding of assorted cultures, history, and theatrical portrayal of the different geographical locations enabled Agatha to incorporate multiple facets into her works. As Agatha accompanied Max for several excavations in the Middle East, she was exposed to the rushes of ancient civilisations and archaeological wonders. This simple exposure offered her immense material and prepared a foundation for her novels and stories, making them praiseworthy. With his knowledge of archaeology, Max allowed Agatha to sharpen her literary skills by exhibiting some of the plots he had sketched, which more than aptly showcased her civilisation-oriented understanding. This collaboration allowed for adequate narrative elements to be incorporated into Agatha's writing. Listed above are a few examples of what can be referred to as inspirational stimuli catering to Agatha's creativity during her life, but there are even more. Not only did her travels provide her with inspiring and diverse cultural practices, traditions and different types of people carved into her imagination deeply, which later inspired her creative endeavour.

Max accompanied Agatha on her extensive trips throughout Europe. Their travels served as an opportunity for archaeological research and to broaden Agatha's view of life. It is clear that the bond they forged further developed Agatha's ability to construct intricate plots within her books. Though Max may not have been the direct inspiration for some of her work, Agatha always seemed to write in a way that made her readers feel he was. Moreover, the feeling of his presence captured in her books alongside her deep romance with him is too precious to be left unexplored. They effortlessly blend vivid imagination with meticulous attention to craftsmanship, breathing life into shapeless ideas through a remarkable synergy of Agatha's spoken fantasies and Max's scholarly intellect.

Mystery and Myth: Incorporating Ancient Legends

Agatha Christie and her husband, Max Mallowan, were archaeologists who explored the myths and legends of the Middle East. The integration of local culture into Christie's literature was deeply inspired by the Middle East's encompassing myths and legends, further supporting the milestones she made in her literary career. Christie drew inspiration from Mesopotamian, Egyptian, and other ancient relics to build the rich tapestries of lost civilisations in her world-famous mysteries, full of enigma and myth. Christie was a gifted author, and every artefact discovered during her and her husband's excavation sparked creativity within her. The powerful mixture of folklore, archaeology, and history provided fertile ground for Christie to plan her intricate plots, which connected with readers across the globe. Her writings were magical because she intertwined ancient mysteries with modern civilisation. She was innovative, and through myths, she captured the interest of countless people worldwide through my novels, breathless with excitement and waiting to turn the pages in professors to ultra mystery novels.

With astute observations and a profound respect for history, she captured the essence of these ancient tales and presented them in mystery and suspense. Thus, her novels were a further testament to her storytelling abilities and became a homage to old myths. In addition, Christie's evocative settings and charismatic characters blended perfectly with the mythical undertones, allowing readers to relive the experiences in bygone ages through distant lands. By incorporating legends into her stories, Christie transformed detective fiction into an examination of ancient myth and mystery. These undeniably striking elements make her works much more profound than simple entertainment. The blend of the past and present, reality and myth, gave her works a deeper significance and gave many readers a novel cultural perspective. In doing so, Agatha Christie became a masterful weaver of literature, hallmarking the pages with boundless imagination intertwined with ancient myths presented in exquisite detail.

Challenges Abroad: Writing Away from Home

For Agatha Christie, writing abroad posed numerous challenges. Each challenge formed a log towards Christie's log of growth in her craft and as an individual. Places such as the Middle East presented Christie with logistical issues like access to essential resources, communication barriers, and even time zones and climate differences. Amid these practical concerns, she also had to balance actively engaging with the cultural vibrance of her surroundings with her writing discipline. The displacement of her preferred writing location forced Christie to change her creative processes. Christie drew inspiration from the landscapes, people, and customs surrounding her, enabling her to create captivating characters and backdrops that still enchant readers today. Further, the lack of Christie's usual support network meant she had to muster immense willpower to stay focused on her craft. She remained connected to the worlds she crafted regardless of the distance, and her writing became a mechanism to bridge the emotional gap to home.

Apart from the travel problems, Christie also had to deal with the imbalance of her adventurous lifestyle and writing. Her travels included strenuous trips and painstaking excavation work with her husband, Max Mallowan, which left little time for writing. Instead of viewing these challenges as obstacles, Christie was able to use them as opportunities to add a real sense of depth to her narratives through her experiences abroad. Christie was able to face these multifaceted challenges and adapt to different places, which greatly increased her creativity. Ultimately, working while she was away from home meant that Christie's literary works gained a more profound global perspective but equally showcased her passion for her work and cemented her legacy as the Queen of Crime.

Conclusion: Outstanding Yet Retained Exotic Allure

Christie's exotic appeal captivates readers due to her creativity and vivid storytelling, including important cultures, lands, and regions. She describes wondrous places very carefully, weaving culture and detail into them. Cases in point are the English countryside, the bustling streets of Istanbul, or even the sun-soaked landscapes of the Middle East, which she describes with such vibrance that it creates memorable images that last beyond the book's last pages.

What separates Christie from other authors is that she captures the character of places and intertwines wonder and mystery with her firsthand observations from those countries. Her travels abroad with her husband, Max Mallowan, inspired most of the stories she wrote. This brings a fresh authenticity and depth to her work. She has captured readers' attention and imagination for decades through routes that transcend culture and boundaries and resonate with the whole world.

In addition, the exotic appeal that has captivated audiences for so long goes beyond the setting. It lies at the very heart of Christie's storytelling. By incorporating local culture, customs, and traditions, Christie gives her tales an air of authenticity and unmatched exotic flair. Her observations and culturally sensitive approach transformed her settings into a feast for the senses, enveloping readers in a world of intrigue.

Moreover, Christie's exotic inspirations further highlight her works' timeless resonance and relevance. Her readers are not only taken back to a different time but also to distant places that remain captivating. Christie's mastery in creating rich, compelling mysteries set against exotic backdrops ensures her works are relevant for years and invite new generations into the magical worlds she created.

Regarding the above, the lasting irresistible charm of Agatha Christie's exoticism narratives speaks to her artistry in portraying the beauty and mystique of distant lands. In her descriptions, insights, and storytelling, Christie created and christened a legacy that still captivates and inspires, which makes her works remain splendid gems adored for their ever-enduring exotic appeal.

8

From Page to Screen

Adapting Agatha for New Audiences

Adaptations

Read Agatha Christie's books; you will appreciate deeply woven plots and compelling characters. People from all over the globe adore her novels. With advancements in technology, Christie's novels have shifted from prose to visual storytelling, which is remarkable. This change is a key point in the literary world, igniting curiosity about the obstacles and achievements of transforming Christie's novels into films. She is perhaps one of the most famous English writers whose works are extensively read. Studying how Agatha Christie's works are being adapted into different media helps one understand why her stories are so appealing and how they change with time. The story of adaptation unfolds with a rich literary society and focuses on how her stories resonate in different cultures and languages. Adaptations spark new levels within the literature, each telling richer stories than the last. It makes this change fascinating because we may focus not only on the content but on how it shifts and performs when told through different forms, especially, in this case, when venturing into the visual realm.

This study is a reverent tribute to the combination of powerful storytelling and adaptation while illustrating the translation of beloved pieces of literature into captivating visual narratives. As we move forward in this journey, we set out to explore the adaptation's intricacies and celebrate Christie's unparalleled impact on the spheres of literature and entertainment.

From Prose to Visuals: Challenges of Translation

The metamorphosis of prose into visuals is a journey filled with a myriad of hurdles in the case of Agatha Christie's literature. Christie's literary world demands a delicate balance of creativity and meticulous detail when transitioning from prose to visual media. One significant challenge that looms large is the task of encapsulating Christie's lifelike characters and her complex plots intricately woven into her prose. The screen adaptation of her works must preserve the trademark suspense that is interwoven through her stories, and for that, every nuance, red herring, and clue must be meticulously transferred, a task that requires unwavering dedication and respect for the original work.

Additionally, changes in the medium require a reconceptualisation of the settings, atmosphere, and ambience. The challenge is to replicate the unique aesthetic of each story accurately and ensure the visual follows along with the vivid imagery spawned from Christie's prose. This task is exceedingly meticulous in detail, accurate in history, and requires understanding the author's intentions.

Also, adapting Christie's works for new audiences provides ample charm that dilutes the original charm and poses significant challenges. The adaptors are forced to grapple with the evolution of social norms, technological advancements, and cultural changes, all while trying to retain the ageless charm of Christie's narratives. It is, in simple terms, a perilous balance of avoiding damage to timeless appeal and modern perspective. This balance is delicate, as it requires the adaptors to respect the original work while also making it relevant and engaging for contemporary audiences.

Striking Christy's dialogue and underlying psychological intricacies from her novels to the screen is equally complicated. It is the battles of wits, social hierarchies, and even friction between characters that need to be portrayed delicately to retain their power in adaptational reproductions as they define the story. These elements are not just plot points, but they are integral to the characters and their development. The nuances involved in portraying the essence of every character's psyche and motivations is underscored by the depth echoing within Christie's writing that demands remarkably challenging storytelling skills.

Amidst the vivid spectrum of show business, "The Agatha Christie Theatre Company" officially holds the trademarks where Christie's captivating theatrical works were brought to life as folk stage productions in various countries. In any part of the globe, Eagle's Eye Theatre had amazing productions from students. These facilities paid careful attention to every detail, right down to the frame of the central part of The Agatha Christie theatre's curtain—sorry, master storyteller.

Analysing Key Adaptations: From Stage to Screen

Agatha is regarded as having inspired over 75 films, counting three unrelated to her works. Now almost all Emmediate Productions have adopted her stories, haggling on a bargain basis and collaborating with her estate. Each of them made historical testaments resurrecting almost android-like poses drowning in aggrandising cinematic narratives based on a montage of Christie's plots with film fables. Nowadays, she provides an endless life-giving constant source for imagination for the children of cyberpunk and traditional animation studios. Her works continue to inspire new generations of artists and storytellers, serving as a rich source of material for creative reinterpretation and adaptation.

Thanks to the transfer from stage to screen, audiences are now able to see every nuance of Christie's mysteries as they unfold in astonishing detail. Adaptations have taken advantage of visual media's features by integrating stunning cinematography and set design to portray Agatha Christie's world compellingly. Additionally, Christie's work has benefited greatly from sound design and musical scoring, which have heightened the tension and drama in her narratives.

In addition, these adaptations have focused on portraying cherished characters like Hercule Poirot and Miss Marple. Filmmakers need to cast actors who capture the traits and mannerisms of the characters so that the transition from page to screen works. As audiences engage with these adaptations, portraying these characters reinvigorates the affection fans hold for them, simultaneously endearing and captivating.

As previously discussed, the transition of a story from stage to screen is a task that comes with the weighty responsibility of simplifying the intricate tales into more digestible versions without losing the essence of the story. In the case of Christie's work, preserving the depth of the plot through the transformation is a complex yet rewarding endeavour. It makes the adaptation both relatable and appealing, and meeting the expectations of the fans as well as those outside the fandom becomes a challenge that requires a high level of artistry and creativity. Directors and screenwriters have strived to capture the essence of Christie's plots using innovative storytelling techniques that involve intricate flashbacks and other non-verbal means, thereby ensuring a captivating experience for the viewers.

As we delve into the analysis of these major adaptations, it becomes evident that the journey from stage to screen has not only polished elements that remain appealing to the viewers but also served as a profound celebration of Agatha Christie's legacy. In the upcoming section, we will immerse ourselves in the iconic portrayals and highlight some of the actors who played significant roles in shaping these cherished characters, a testament to the enduring influence of Christie's work.

Iconic Portrayals: Actors Breathing Life into Characters

In adaptations of Agatha Christie's works, the portrayal of characters is part and parcel of the attempt to bring her stories to life on screens. In adherence to honouring Christie's work, the actors chosen to play these characters are important because they must be able to portray them convincingly.

There are several portrayals in the history of Agatha Christie adaptations that have been done well and that have impressed a lot of viewers. One of these includes David Suchet's portrayal of Hercule Poirot in the long-running television series 'Agatha Christie's Poirot' which, alongside contemporaneous adaptations of Poirot novels, is praised for capturing all of the whip's Poirot habits and manners Christie describes in her books. Indeed, Suchet's exhaustive portrayal of Poirot's habits and his understanding of the character won the performer both accolades and scorn, but appreciation from readers of the literary works was overwhelming.

Other than that, Joan Hickson and Geraldine McEwan are other actresses who played Miss Marple and made remarkable incarnations of the character whilst remaining faithful to her spirit and character.

The importance of primary characters aside, supporting characters have contributed greatly to Agatha Christie's stories. From the charming Captain Hastings, who assists Poirot, to the mysterious Mr. Satterthwaite in Tales of Harley Quin, these supporting characters add value to Christie's world.

Actors have the task of bringing to life characters created from the multi-faceted tapestry of Agatha Christie. The distinctive traits, what drives them, and the ethical complexities of the characters about whom stories are told are taken to a whole new level by the performers, achieving far greater than what adaptation in purely visual form would entail.

In some situations, certain parts can be so adored that an adaptation permanently shifts the character's perception. This was the case when the ever-talented Kenneth Branagh played the iconic role of Hercule Poirot in 'Murder on the Orient Express' in 2017. Along with the golden aura surrounding the role, Branagh had the opportunity to present his interpretation of the famed detective, thus allowing his audiences to revisit Poirot while enjoying all the modern aspects brought to the timeless character.

As we examine the adaptations of Agatha Christie's works, it is striking how actors portray her characters, reflecting how powerful her stories are. These adaptations guarantee that

Agatha Christie's spirit lives on, ensuring her legacy continues even in visual interpretations, where she is known as the "Queen of Crime."

Creative Liberties: Balancing Fidelity and Innovation

Each of Christie's novels and stories is timeless, which presents a challenge. It requires finding a balance between honouring and paying respect to the content and creating reinterpretations that capture the imagination of all audiences. Adaptations that incorporate new elements most strongly require a grasp of the source material alongside innovative approaches to capture the rest of the viewers.

In preserving a character's distinctiveness, Christie's intricate plots and distinctive characters are essential if one wishes to preserve fidelity. Changes require balancing the core of her narratives with the need to freshen them up for modern audiences. In this case, adaptation does not mean incomplete freedom—one must follow and pay great attention to detail while honouring the author's original work, intention, style, and approach.

But equally important is innovation in adapting Christie's tales for contemporary audiences. Adapters add new perspectives to familiar stories, which require changing character relationships, settings, and sometimes even the whole narrative. These adaptations oscillate between tradition and update, simultaneously respecting and modernising Christie's compelling mysteries.

One sociocultural characteristic with which Christie's mysteries are framed is the balance between gender and social hierarchy interactions. Christie's contemporaries would be inclined to consider these changes, but they would humorously offer sympathetic voices or alternative narratives to dominant societal norms actively silencing characters in Christie's stories. This approach not only enriches the stories but also allows for important discussions about the portrayal of people through narratives.

Innovation also shows itself in how the adaptations are done visually and aurally. Film and television adaptations strive to capture the sophisticated worlds in which Christie's narratives take place through a thorough approach to cinematography, sound design, and production design, thereby enhancing the viewer's experience while preserving the original work's essence.

Additionally, modern adaptations use advanced technologies, such as digital effects and multimedia, to intricately elaborate on layers of a narrative. These innovations broaden the scope of creativity, but care is taken to ensure that Christie's effortless elegance remains the focus.

In the final analysis, balancing fidelity and innovation in adapting Agatha Christie's works requires both appreciating the depth of her literary corpus and having the creative boldness to transform timeless classics. This balance guarantees that new audiences continue to experience the enchantment of Christie's stories, ensuring her relevance across eras.

Global Reach: Navigating Cultural Transitions

The works of Agatha Christie have achieved a global reach since they are unique to every culture. There is always the problem of cultural adaptation when her works are integrated into different cultures. There is an adaptation of almost every single one of her books, and translating them involves a complex interplay of etiquette and societal norms. The cultural puzzles that shaped Christie's stories for international audiences needed deep understanding, careful research, and an appreciation for the peculiarities of each culture. Knowing how different the attitudes toward crime, mystery, and justice are in various parts of the world is equally important.

Understanding how different cultures perceive the nuances of language and history is crucial in navigating these cultural transitions. The involvement of numerous collaborators is instrumental in maintaining the cultural authenticity of the characters' interactions. This raises a fundamental question: How do different cultures engage with characters and their responses? These efforts are not only vital for comprehending Christie's work, but also for adapting it for presentation and acceptance in diverse societies worldwide.

Audience immersion is made simple through highly successful cross-cultural adaptations carefully tailored to respect sociocultural frameworks. These adaptations work on local and regional levels, integrating society's customs and traditions. They enable people to encapsulate the essence of differing cultures and appreciate the underlying conflicts and emotions that transcend people from various cultures.

Cultural transitions allow the original narratives to be deepened through the infusion of new insights and perspectives. Frameworks that foster diversity and inclusion help revive Christie's classic works, making them adaptable to a transforming world while ensuring their enduring relevance. A careful approach to cultural differences enhances global storytelling while preserving Agatha Christie's legacy for years to come.

Modern Retellings: Engaging New Generations

Storytelling is an art that requires reworking for different cultures and generations. Christie's stories have been retold for contemporary viewers, where traditions are blended with modern expectations. These adaptations strike a delicate balance between the originality of Christie's works and the contemporary appeal necessary to engage today's viewers. In modern retellings like 'Pale Horse' and 'ABC Murders, the viewers are captivated and provoked using contemporary means of sight and narrative. The adaptations do not aim to replicate the original works; rather, there is an intent to reimagine them. This is achieved by using strong conceptual frameworks to draw the attention of the new generation. Moreover, in order to cater to the new audience, there is an intention to employ high-end technology and production values for an aesthetic that meets modern standards. By respecting the legacy of the original text while committing to contemporary innovation, Christie's stories continue to live on through her adaptations, which are now presented for discerning audiences.

Moreover, these modern interpretations offer opportunities to engage with themes and characters through a contemporary lens, igniting reflections and conversations on the unending aspects of human nature, morality, and justice. Modern retellings serve a dual purpose in this blend of the past and present: paying tribute to the cornerstones of Christie's narratives while incorporating them into today's society. In this light, these adaptations help to maintain the relevance of Christie's works, enabling her stories to remain meaningful to numerous future generations.

Critical Reception: How Adaptations Stand the Test of Time

Like most other literary ones, Christie's adaptations face the brunt of harsh scrutiny for not capturing the originality in her complex plots and characters. The reviews of these adaptations have often debated the fine line between respecting the source material and attempting to enliven it for modern audiences. As with any other artwork, criticism of Christie's adaptations tends to focus greatly on the decisions made by film directors, screenwriters, and even actors portraying her fictional characters.

The depiction of well-known characters such as Hercule Poirot and Miss Marple is always a prominent observation. Iconic characters demonstrate different traits and mannerisms in Christie's novels; hence, there is great anticipation for their adaptation on screen. Traditionally, critics analyse how actors performing these roles are remarked upon. It is also noted that an actor's performance is almost always bound to be compared with his predecessors or later contemporaries. In addition, the depiction of Christie's stories marked by complexity and astonishing revelations within a particular 'scope' of storytelling becomes a point of criticism. Adaptations are critiqued and reviewed based on how well they recreate the spirit of suspense and intrigue, the hallmark of Christie's writing.

Equally important are the other elements of visual presentation and aesthetic artistry because these form the basis of the adaptation review. Each camera shot, set, and costume are building blocks in adapting and interpreting Christie's words into visual form. Critics assess how well these elements guide and pave the way for the audience to experience the environment in which the stories take place. Also very important, using accurate dates and detailed history goes a long way in preserving the charm and authenticity of Christie's stories.

Another key aspect noted by reviewers of adaptations is the consideration given to plot twists and resolutions. Adaptations are placed under severe scrutiny evaluating whether they maintain the shock value of Christie's clever and unorthodox endings. Reviewers pay a great deal of attention to the suspense, rising action, and resolution of striking turning points and milestones, stressing the importance of maintaining the tension, which is integral to the works of Christie. This emphasis on tension keeps the audience engaged and eager to see how the story unfolds.

Additionally, the impacts of adaptation over time and its relevance remain a widely debated focal point among critics. Undoubtedly, it is difficult to assess how modern an audience's expectations regarding relevance alongside Christie's timeless narrative can be. It becomes frustrating when an attempt is made to discover what aspects of these adaptations allow them to survive in the ever-changing paradigm of cinema.

Adapting Christie's works to different forms of media is not without its challenges. Each medium has its own unique constraints and opportunities, and adapting a story from one to another requires careful consideration of these factors. Ultimately, Christie's adaptations underscore the importance of honouring the author's ideas while trying to appeal to wider audiences. Adaptations that strive to sustain Christie's unparalleled styles pay tribute to her, but at the same time claim her reign in the world of visual retelling, signifying the true divergence of her narratives adapted to different forms of media.

Impact on Christie's Legacy: Editors Weigh In

Shifting Christie's works across different platforms will, without a doubt, affect her legacy as a writer. Every editor looks back at her adaptations and, in their way, articulates the impact she has had and is still having in literature. As tellers of stories, Christie's adaptations will always be relevant, timeless, and in demand.

The patrons of an author's estate, in most cases the editors, have to strike a deal between preserving a legacy and presenting it in a manner that speaks to today's culture. Christie's editors, in particular, understand how her books have been translated into films and how the readers and audience reception, which has more or less influenced the dynamics around her work, has been critical.

In speaking with Ago, the editors have noted that her mysteries have been transformed into films and her novels turned into stage plays or musicals. They express their admiration for the creativity seen in adaptations and fear of oversimplifying the original texts. They focus on the storyline, character development, and the delicate placement of clues in her tales and mysteries wrapped in travel guides, termed novels, that together form the whodunit genre. Additionally, they point out the balancing act of preserving originality while adding something fresh to appeal to contemporary standards.

How effective adaptations have brought to life a new audience of readers and viewers of Christie's novels, captured during a specific period, is how these editors comment on the shift. They point out that the adaptations have, indeed, retained the fundamental principles of her storytelling and, at the same time, reinvigorated interest towards her extensive works. Moreover, they highlight the cycle of adaptations and sustained popularity of her novels, which keeps bringing new fans from various places worldwide.

These conversations make it apparent that bringing Christie's works to diverse audiences is a collective effort that involves editors, producers, and other creative professionals, revealing new layers of collaboration. The ways editors shaped contemporary interpretations of Christie's complexioned works showcase how adaptations impact enduring literary influence to a greater scope. They depict a dominating triple stranglehold of addiction to her stories with the charismatic, timeless, and ingenious string of words penned down to weave her imagination.

When looking through the eyes of the hired editors, it is clear that the adapted versions of Christie's works remain in circulation as they both honour her legacy and help propagate the transcendental allure of her stories for decades. Their observations show that Christie's mastery of narrative continues to be unparalleled, showcasing elements of her uncanny ability for timeless mystique captivating even beyond death for centuries to come.

Conclusion: Adapting Agatha for Future Audiences

After finishing the analysis of Agatha's captivating life and the adaptations associated with her, it is clear that modern viewers hold on to the allure of Christie's works because they seem to transcend narratives of time. The elegance in craftsmanship, intricacy of the plots, and character development created by

Christie showcase her talent in crafting masterpieces; her work, regardless of innumerable adaptations or interpretations, remains unchallenged.

In pursuing modernising and bringing Agatha Christie's literature to future audiences, it is essential to balance accessibility and contemporising. Editors and other creatives working on these adaptations face the challenge of preserving Christie's brilliance while tailoring her work to modern audiences and shifting societal perspectives.

Advanced technology comes with its own form of entertainment. The issue presented will be finding timeless Christie mysteries that appeal to the modern audience. Unlike in the past, technology today presents a plethora of opportunities to repurpose classic stories by fueling them with inviting forms of storytelling, exciting visual tricks, and captivating elements that appeal to veteran admirers alongside fresh viewers.

Thanks to her eminent storytelling, Christie's work does not require extensive marketing strategies to reach international audiences. Their global popularity has spotlighted the dynamic portrayal of multiple cultures in Agatha Christie's adaptations. However, it should also be attempted to ensure that Christie's underlying ideas and messages remain prominent and adapt to many cultures inclusively without losing the universality of her concepts.

However, for now, Christie's adaptations provide great potential towards unknown audiences and modern-day generations to impact contemporary culture and introduce them to sophisticated storytelling. Such adaptations sustain Christie's legacy and enable her claim to be a constant influence for people of all ages, cultures, and storytellers worldwide.

9

The Vanishing Act

Christie's Own Life Mystery

Prelude to Disappearance: Setting the Stage

Christie's fame and career peaked when she mysteriously vanished in 1926. Agatha Mary Clarissa Christie was born in 1890 in the English coastal town of Torquay. Christie was a novelist, dramatist, and short-story writer with exceptional titles like 'Murder on the Orient Express' and Christie's Forensic, which made her stand out as a brilliant writer in the fiction genre. Like many people, Christie's professional life is filled with achievements, while her personal life is plagued with difficulties. These included the First World War, her first husband's divorce, and the strife of maintaining her reputation as a writer. As her literary career picked up steam, Christie struggled to meet the balancing expectations of her readers and the publishing industry. Her personal life's mounting pressures and complexities created a clash that changed the public's interest. They simultaneously set the stage to quiet the world with the spellbinding escape of the Queen of Crime. The events before her disappearance blended her professional commitments and personal unrest that heightened the suspense of Christie's life.

Analysing Agatha's life highlights why the complexity of her character and internal conflicts might have shaped the next eccentric incident in the timeline.

A Sudden Vanishing: The Day She Went Missing

Agatha's sudden disappearance on December 3, 1926, was a day that shook the world, a tragic and unexpected event. The distinct placement and scenography of her life as a missing writer stirred controversy alongside media attention, spiralling into a literary and international disaster with her vanishing at the epicentre. She did not intend to escape her reality unlike what people in sauntering hope offer; the frenzied tendrils of the media levelled blame everywhere while attempting to grasp hold of answers to aid in the frantic writing of counter articles. The missing author's last wisely trailing pieces of prose were scattered across her home, waiting to bite back but unable to escape. The entire country had their attention remarkably fixated on her schemes and plans as the intrigue hidden within her life unfolded, but forgot to realise how it had temporarily perished. Answers streamed freely, conjured from wild speculation alongside ample reasoning; flanked by an endless bout of publicity. All these factors together in turn revolving around the incident set her life in turmoil, jumping the boundaries within hopes that she would push beyond the herculean effort sparked by her backdrop. As newspapers received peeks into the vanish, every detail captivated attention while experts threw themselves into concrete turmoil, all momentum built led her to lose steam, epic relief thrust forth alongside tension waiting to lock up with each turn.

The Public Frenzy: Media and Search Operations

The alarming chain of events which seized the public's attention and media passions was set into motion by Agatha Christie's sudden disappearance on the evening of December 3, 1926. Every newspaper had Agatha's disappearance on the front page. During this period, Agatha was a famous author. Her disappearance from public life brought attention from correspondents far and wide. A gossip frenzy began, which overshadowed the actual location where she went.

Christie's disappearance made the general populace worry about her well-being. Friends, family, and admirers sympathised with her family, which eventually made the publicity too overwhelming. Alas, her disappearance garnered widespread publicity. Her family began to face immense public scrutiny. Loosely translated, DIY investigators and properly trained detectives began to assist in the search. The media immediately noticed the mystery and began using it as fresh content.

Instruments of the media were eagerly aiding the hunt for framing speculation around her disappearance. Each person had their take on the disappearance; some leaned more towards vague belief while others built their world around it. She was not only missing; Christie was missing for reporters, too. There was conjecture from every side; the country was taken by storm. When this controversy was occurring, the mystery of Christie's disappearance had grown in the public interest more than ever before. Reporters and newspapers seemed to go overboard covering Christie's case, and as mandated, it became a spectacle for the entire nation. Consequently, the concern and anxiety regarding the author's updates highlighted the degree to which her disappearance had affected the people.

With all the strong media focus and speculation around the author, the search for Agatha Christie continued with unwavering determination. Her disappearance became the focus of an entire nation, drawing in both volunteers and concerned citizens. Day after day, this collaborative chase sustained momentum, fueled by the forceful efforts of law enforcement, which turned the collective goal into a community-wide mission.

The Unfolding Mystery: Clues and Speculations

Numerous theories and hints that only furthered the mystery are underlying the fountain of pandemonium created by Christie's vanishing act. Her case became a phenomenon drawing people from all walks of life, leaving no stone unturned. Her belief in the final location in the car and the car itself compelled both officials and the public to join forces.

Various theories began circulating, and there were uncalled-for assumptions about why Christie went missing. Some hypothesised mishap, claiming someone abducted her, while others thought it was self-inflicted as a means to garner attention towards her novels. Personal issues coupled with outside forces sometimes led to assumptions regarding her decision to go off the grid.

All these assumptions made winnowing actionable hints from purposeless mystery drags quite taxing. Nevertheless, devoted detectives left no stone unturned, ready to spend time and effort gathering data and connecting the dots to reach a conclusion.

Suspicious situations surrounding Christie's disappearance led to huge manhunts conducted by the police along with volunteers and locals. Every piece of information, temperamental or serious, contributed to the growing mystique of Christie's disappearance alongside her absence.

The ever-changing tale of the mystery waiting to unfold kept the viewers hooked. Sensationalist news companies exacerbated the problem by providing misleading coverage and feeding the existing lie to the public, allowing more easily manipulatable information to enter the already complicated situation.

Even as the frenzy played out, the timeless inquiry continued to burn: What prompted Agatha Christie's unanticipated retreat from public attention? While there were many hypotheses, tangible solutions were still missing, leaving the globe confused about the spellbinding moment when the truth would be revealed.

Unraveling the Enigma: Discovery and Consequences

The mystery of Agatha Christie captured worldwide interest, which included the public and government, as every lead was investigated. Christie's disappearance had deep underlying effects that provoked worry, intense debate, and even borderline hysteria. While journalists tried to get all the information available, the literary world closely followed the incidents, with almost disbelief in witnessing reality unfold before them. The discovery of Agatha's car only made the mystery deeper. Her vanishing act took centre stage and became the topic of discussion not only amongst Romantics but also tore apart her personal life and literary legacy. Regardless of the decades she had spent writing such limbs of words, the sudden mystery brought many questions to light and exposed the frail strings she was hanging onto. The sophisticated existence of public outlooks alongside the intricate web of struggles remains unanswered. The collective mystery that puzzled the world and involved harsh conclusions left them wondering all alone. The truth behind the mystery does not solely rely on one woman's disappearance; her engulfing growth in fame and existence pushes societal expectations, too. When the discovery of Agatha's whereabouts was made, there was a sense of burning curiosity mixed with relief, allowing everyone to confront so many questions left unanswered in the wild.

The lingering effects her return would have will shape her tale and transform the readers' view of this writer and the enigmatic tales she wove.

Behind the Curtain: Agatha's Account and Confession

Fancy disappearing without a trace? Agatha's life proves that life can be more picturesque than any fiction book for a split moment. In late December of 1926, Agatha disappeared without a single note or word to anyone. Selflessly, hundreds of eager volunteers explored every nook and cranny in search of Agatha while the media relentlessly bombarded her family's home with intrusive questions. After everything, all the buzz turned out to be nothing; in the end, she was at a Harrogate hotel waiting for someone to figure out she was gone. While the world outside was missing a page and burdened with myths, she lived the best of both worlds. Unique speculation inundated everyone's mind, including the simple fact that Christie was buckling under the weight of an alternate identity. Once everything settled down and chaos relinquished, she shared a novel-like description of her baffling actions and an astonishing confession. By her account, her life seemed broken and zeroed out - aka unfathomable stress. The accompanying nonsense added to her tedious lifestyle and a golden touch called social life. She truly was living a celebrity's nightmare. In detailed consensus, she did create one remarkable confession that suddenly baffled everyone from haters to believers to sympathisers - her meltdown surely painted a patriotic portrait of the unclaimed vendetta over the life of celebrities.

While revealing the inner turmoil and the conflict that preceded her disappearing act, readers appreciated her character and creative works more nuancedly. This revelation explains the unique synergy between lived experiences and narrative crafting, illustrating the multifaceted relationship between a storyteller's life and their work. Christie's contrition sheds light on the vulnerable side of creativity, highlighting the burdens of emotional strain within the woman's imagination, which radically transforms the logic of suffering. Frustrating as it may sound, laurel wreaths of imagination devour their suggestive ground. Additionally, her willingness to grapple with her demons is relatable and serves to empathise with other readers and creators within the arts and literature. For all these reasons, Agatha Christie's account and confession offer a striking depiction that goes beyond fiction, exploring the captivating complexities of the human experience.

Psychological Insights: The Mind of a Storyteller

The world of literature was shocked in 1926 when Agatha Christie mysteriously disappeared. She was a prominent writer known for her creativity, which raises as many questions as it provides answers. The complexities behind Christie's psyche require one to indulge in a detailed analysis of her narrative abilities and perspective on the world. Christie's remarkable writing skills stemmed from her exceptional comprehension of human nature, behaviour, and interactions. Her keen understanding and observation of human actions, sentiments, and motives aided her in crafting her iconic characters, elaborate plots, and nuanced, multilayered stories. These arguments make sense in light of the motivations that caused her enigmatic disappearance. Christie's mind offers a unique perspective where nearly endless possibilities reside, and a delicate balance exists between reality, imagination, and personal adventures. Such a perspective exposes raw vulnerability, revealing a paradoxical battle for inspiration fuelled by the need to create change. Studying Christie's creative process through a psychological lens showcases a powerful blend of empathy, imagination, and emotional truth, which is waiting to unfold as women and men navigate the world towards self-realisation. In addition, examining Christie's life highlights the changes that shifted her reality, and the stories that stem from such shifts showcase the evolution of ideas and coherence in her life.

When a reader starts exploring the intricate passages of

Agatha Christie's mind, they are met with an exciting blend of creativity, bold emotions, and intellect. Christie, wholeheartedly and passionately, possessed the unparalleled gift of critiquing the perplexing human experience by shaping it into captivating stories that still echo through time. The authenticity of her characters set them apart from the rest due to the psychological plausibility that underscored her prologue, which represents the iconic works of literature she composed. Christie's literary prowess places her among the geniuses of literature, due to her unrivalled talent in revealing the clean locked doors of man's psyche, and explaining the many layered phenomena alongside it. Therefore, gauging and reasoning the psychological subtleties crafted in the brain of a narrator turns out to be very fundamental in understanding the deep impact Christie has had on literature, as well as the complexity surrounding her captivating figure. Her work continues to resonate with readers and scholars, transcending time and remaining as relevant today as it was when it was first written.

Analysing Motives: Personal Pressures and Fame

The disappearance of Agatha Christie in 1926 brought her motives into sharp focus, especially considering the personal pressures and resultant fame that surrounded her. The public's perception of Christie significantly shaped the context of her personal and professional identity. Given the success of her literary works and the public's expectations, she faced a tremendous amount of stress to balance and maintain her personal life. Earning fame as a novelist, she must have faced enormous pressure to creatively maintain her standing as a 'Queen of Crime.' This was the time when Christie was coming to grips with the overwhelming nature of celebrity, which had a massive impact on her emotional health. More personal issues like the ending of her first marriage and some financial difficulties added to the burden of stored pressure. It is reasonable to argue that these circumstances combined in her mind to give rise to some internal mental conflicts culminating in the decision to disappear. Christie's narrative is a compelling testament to the challenges of unprecedented fame juxtaposed with creative ability and psychological endurance, a struggle that many can relate to.

In addition, the complex nature of fame, which is popularly perceived as luxurious, can serve as an extremely difficult test for an individual's mental strength and ethics. This reflection on fame and its pressure stimulates Christie's life and artistic legacy. Addressing the reason for her disappearance helps us explore the intensity of controversy surrounding identity and fame, where personal struggles stand in opposition to acknowledgement. Her complex story intertwined with universal truths resonates with countless readers and scholars, appealing to a deeper invitation into human mystery. Christie's work delves into the human condition, exploring areas of turmoil and acclaim, leading to a conflict that deeply fascinates readers and scholars. In her story, we can still discover glimpses of what deepens Christie's relevance beyond time, teaching hints of the fierce pursuit of integrity and mastery over creations.

Legacy of the Vanishing Act: Impact on Her Works

The enigma surrounding Agatha Christie's disappearance in 1926 adds an undeniable allure to Christie's personal life and her works. Without a trace during the disappearance, France called her missing, and she became a national sensation. Agatha Christie underwent apparent social shifts in addition to the concealed changes; the profound nature of her work shifted with narrative style and thematic elements in her novels. Breaking away from the public eye altered Christie's temporally altered state, which seemed to flow into her writing, deepening the experience.

Christie's later life works demonstrated her increasing interest in the psychology surrounding mysteries of disappearance, including motives for committing such actions. Her unique case was one of the many sources of inspiration for multiple plots centred around missing people, secret motives, and concealed realities. This was when some of her best-crafted and most deeply psychological mysteries were born, adding to the literary world classics that remain popular.

Furthermore, the mystery of her disappearing act did not limit itself to the boundaries of her fictional works. It reached the public sphere, which helped cement her identity as an incredible woman shrouded in the charm of mystique. The mystery of her disappearance and her life's work drew unprecedented public attention, furthering the intrigue surrounding her identity.

Also, the consequences of her disappearance affected the entire spectrum of detective fiction, and her mastery of suspense and misdirection was only emulated in later works by other authors. The novels published after Christie's disappearance contained intricate plotting and unexpected twists; these set a precedent that defined the framework of story development for aspiring writers.

To sum up, Agatha Christie's legacy and the enigma of her life and works, perpetuated by her disappearance, add an indelible mark on the literary world, specifically in mystery fiction. It endures throughout time as many of her readers grapple with timeless literary brilliance, making boundless boundaries cease to exist.

Reflections: Piecing Together the Truth

Reflecting on Agatha Christie's mysterious disappearance leads to the conclusion that it greatly affected her personal life and literary works. The truth behind the disappearance is still unsolved, and digging deeper gives a perspective of human nature in contrast to the creative process of an artist.

After Christie's dramatic return, she did not give any statement regarding her disappearance, which has resulted in endless theories, including amnesia and a well-orchestrated publicity stunt. These claims only further complicate her legacy, which is superhero-like in nature yet enigmatic, showing complex real-life motivations behind her art.

The mysteriously transformative years of her life were an inspiration during her time as an author, as potential identity crises that accompanied secrets and thriving deception mark the literary world's contemporaries' hallmark. This personal turmoil was bound to happen, reflecting jarring themes in Christie's stories, such as loss, illusion, and the paradox of existence.

The lasting ramifications of Agatha's mysterious disappearance demonstrate the essential link between an author's life and their work, once again highlighting the crossover between reality and fiction. Life events, and in her case, disappearances, create complex narrative arcs and character development unique to her stories. The unchanged mystery of her disappearance speaks surely to the essence of this phenomenon, along with the hidden truths behind a writer's mind.

As we strive to uncover the reason behind her disappearance, we are, one way or another, forced to explore the wide range of reasons behind an author's image and work. Each narrative of an author's life weaves in rich, complex realities, truth tangled among imagination. From this episode, the lessons to take from it are innumerable: more often than not, the distinction between boundaries of reality and fiction is profoundly obscured, and authors' stories often bear traces of their fundamentally unfathomable lives. Christie's disappearing act is beyond just depicting a gap in history—rather, it addresses an entire mysterious paradox, inviting us to challenge fundamental mystique storytelling creators.

10

A Lasting Impact

The Legacy of the Queen of Crime

Christie's Enduring Legacy

Christie's A Touch Of Deceit: An Agatha Christie Mystery, a calligraphed document under a literary lock, for example, has left an indelible mark on the world of literature, a mark that continues to grow in influence over modern crime fiction. Her legacy, which spans generations, speaks to the timeless themes of human consciousness and the art of deception. By focusing on the extent of Christie's contributions, we can better understand the enduring change she has brought to the fabric of modern crime fiction. The evolution she initiated shines brightly through Christie's works, captivating writers to this day with the striking strokes of her trademarked brush, masterfully evoking logic.

Influence on Modern Crime Fiction Authors

Agatha Christie's legacy and work still affect modern crime fiction authors through her psychological thrillers and mysteries. Her work shaped the genre due to her unique methods in storytelling, bounding characterisation, and weaving multi-faceted plots. They strive to accomplish what she mastered: writing suspense, ingenious plot twists, and the art of building tension.

Many claim that Christie served as their main source of influence, showcasing Christie's impactful legacy in today's literature. This impact is evident with Ruth Rendell, P. D. James, and Tana French openly stating that Christie's work affected their crime dramas. They all employ Christie's trademark elements, such as the mastermind behind the murder, complex archetypes, and unconventional use of red herrings and misdirection. These techniques, which involve misleading the reader or viewer to divert attention from the real culprit, are used by these authors to propel the plot forward.

Equally important, Christie's acute understanding of human nature and the skilful development of various characters serve as examples for writers who wish to add complexity and depth to their works. Christie's contribution to crime fiction remains unparalleled due to her psychological and multi-dimensional character motivations and emotionally complex hidden agendas that forever changed storytelling in the genre. It has become the norm to clinically analyse characters and moral paradoxes within the multi-layered fabric of contemporary crime fiction.

Furthermore, Christie's impact on the genre is evident in the changing portrayal of detectives and sleuths in modern crime fiction. Her unforgettable creations, such as Hercule Poirot and Miss Marple, have not only astounded readers but also inspired modern prose to craft great, traditional, and often eccentric reasoning detectives. Christie's legacy continues to inspire the creation of new detectives, cleverly puzzling and intellectually complex, unlike any before.

In summary, Agatha Christie's impact on contemporary crime novel writers goes beyond imitation, as her legacy lives within the very heart of the genre. Christie will always remain a unique figure through her storytelling, characters, and narratives, which continue to resonate with modern crime fiction to this day.

Christie's Works in Academic Circles

Agatha Christie's novels have received considerable admiration in academic circles, placing her as one of the best and most important literary figures. Academics have worked on her books, novels, or any other literature, as well as her characters and story techniques. Many papers, publications, research work, and conferences that have polished crime fiction have explored Christie's weaving of intricate themes, plots, clues, and red herrings. An exemplary example includes gaping holes in Christie's impact on shaping crime fiction. The testimony of her fictional detective novels and her novels in broader domains of literature have been studied closely through the prism of Christie's legacy and impact. Furthermore, the analysis of Christie's works illustrates the penetrating observations she made about people and human behaviour, ways in which people examine her works in the context of psychological frameworks analysis to highlight motives and human deception and the intricacies of human nature within the world of her literature. Christie paved the way for theories and discourse, surpassing known boundaries and archetypes of literary structure, making her the centrepiece of sociopolitical dialogue and critical literary analysis.

In addition, Christie's works have richly served interdisciplinary studies due to the depth and diversity of themes ranging from social commentary to explorations of morality and justice. These themes explore the multidimensional nature of her storytelling. Christie's influence in the academic world stretches far beyond English literature departments. Her works are taught in criminology, psychology, sociology, and cultural studies, making her narratives Christaic case studies for human behaviour, social constructs, and the interplay of law and morality. Including Agatha Christie's works in the academic curriculum reflects the enduring literary value of her work while also highlighting Christie's literature as important intellectual resources that provoke discussions on many aspects of humanity.

The Global Reach and Cultural Impact of Her Novels

Christie's cultural impact delineates the reach of her literary works, which date back to Agatha Christie's life. It is no surprise that Christie is dubbed 'The Queen of Crime' as her intricately woven mysteries with taut plots rich in character have earned her accolades across the globe. Hercule Poirot and Miss Marple are some of Christie's iconic detectives who have earned Christie immense recognition. Her intricate works have been translated into various languages, ensuring a plethora of readers have access to them. The novels featuring Christie's iconic characters mark her prominence in literature, enhancing cultural exchange and uniting avid readers from various backgrounds. As a sharp observer of human nature, it can be said that Christie's understanding of sociocultural context was uncanny, which deepened the understanding and increased empathy towards humans across different cultures. Besides literature, Christie's works heavily influence other popular forms of entertainment. Numerous films, TV shows, plays, and yes, even video games have referenced, parodied, and reimagined many of her characters as well as plotlines, which only goes to show the prevailing impact of her work: Christie's claim of being a crime queen is justified which further marks the enduring touchstones of culture.

Moreover, the many appearances of Christie's work in popular culture have aided in the archival and continuation of her narratives so that new audiences always interact with her stories. Her work is a powerful means of transnational intercultural communication, promoting sentiment among people who sometimes do not share the same living space but appreciate her work. Her novels have inspired many tourist attractions and events, marking her literary legacy and drawing admirers from different countries, which, to some extent, indicates the cultural importance of her works. The enthusiasm with which they participate confirms the depth of the fact that her stories are appreciated and valued around the world.

Adaptations and Their Role in Reviving Interest

The works of Agatha Christie have been popular and continue to do so because of the many adaptations done in different forms of art, such as television series, stage plays, and blockbuster films. Some of her captivating narratives have also been transformed successfully, bringing them to the attention of people who have not heard of them before. These adaptations have worked towards modernising the classic works, quote-unquote, ensuring that Christie's legacy keeps flourishing within popular culture.

Adaptations can change the story's perspective and allow the audience to explore different themes and ideas. People are now able to view the most cherished stories from a different lens, which ultimately instigates new conversations and critiques. Adaptation efforts can further bring Christie's robust narratives to a younger audience, guaranteeing that her legacy will live on for many years. By using engaging visuals and creative sound, captivating a wider audience can be achieved to prove that Christie's works are ageless, leading to her vines as a literary legend.

In addition, adaptations prove Christie's narratives' agelessness and universality, ensuring their relevance in shifting cultural tides.

These adaptations concern a wide range of audiences because they incorporate contemporary aspects alongside classic features, and in turn, they have received overwhelming acclaim while perpetuating Christie's literary fame. In this manner, these adaptations are crucial in preserving and disseminating Christie's incomparable legacy, telling stories so that her everlasting impact on the world's literary landscape is sustained for the future. Adapted works, perhaps, have the most profound effects since they continually add to the enduring fascination with Christie's intricate lines and enigmatic personas, captivating audiences with every version and sparking renewed interest in the exceptional craftsmanship of the Queen of Crime.

Literary Awards and Posthumous Recognitions

The numerous awards and recognitions Agatha Christie

achieved during her lifetime, and those she received after her death for her literary works, cement her position as 'Queen of Crime'. The huge effect that Christie had in detective fiction was and still is acclaimed worldwide and was even awarded on multiple occasions. She was given awards like the Edgar Award, which is considered a mark of great achievements in the field and is named after a well-known figure in mysteries and thrillers, Edgar Allan Poe. Along with those, the compelling narratives and ingenious storytelling techniques were considered reason enough for her to be awarded The Grand Master Award by the Mystery Writers of America. She was the first to win it, making it more special. The award is more or less an indicator of how much Christie's work means to the literary world. Moreover, the impact of Christie's works is not limited to one place, which speaks for why she was able to join the Detection Club, a private society made of renowned crime writers that is only accessible to a select few, giving her recognition in the detective fiction industry.

Christie's talent for constructing detailed plots and characters enabled her to produce literary works with such utter promptness that it earned her a Dame Commander of the Order of the British Empire. Even after her death, she is still remembered for her contributions to literature, such as awards that have been named after her, which is a testament to her lasting legacy. These include the Agatha Awards, which honour achievements in traditional mystery and crime writing and are given out by Malice Domestic every year, further commemorating Christie's impact on literature. In addition, the Agatha Christie Festival was established to celebrate her contributions to literature and the mystery genre in particular. Year after year, literary awards bestowed in her name further immortalise Christie's significance in literature, proving that her impact reaches beyond periods and ages. The countless adaptations and sales of Agatha Christie's remarkable pieces demonstrate her lasting influence in the world of crime fiction, alongside numerous awards and accolades given in her honour.

Christie's Contribution to Literary Techniques

They say that crime doesn't pay, but Agatha Christie proves otherwise. From her innovative twists and turns to her intricate puzzles, Christie has forever changed the landscape of crime fiction and all forms of literature. Every author draws inspiration from somewhere, but Christie's literature is the starting point for many in the crime fiction genre. Her astounding ability to weave life's nuanced details into plots filled with cliffhangers showcases Christie's attention to detail in her work. Readers can immerse themselves in story worlds rich with depth through Christie's portrayal of complex characters. Each character hides something deeply ingrained within their persona, allowing Christie to create multifaceted plots and riddles. Her mastery doesn't end there, however. Her deep understanding of human psychology elevates her from being a mere mystery novelist; Christie becomes a genius who infuses intricate insights into life encapsulated in a single whodunit.

By analysing her characters' psyche, she transforms traditional mystery novels into captivating narratives. On top of that, the way she highlights social issues and merges them with her stories underlines the author's genius and her understanding of societal dynamics. Christie's work gives timeless relevance to literature that has yet to be fully appreciated.

Christie's acute understanding of human nature and her skill of blending these attributes into fascinating stories have made her mesmerising mysteries that continue to fascinate readers of all ages. Her life's work for sharpening the tools and techniques of crime fiction undoubtedly remains unrivalled and offers enduring inspiration for emerging authors, thereby influencing writing culture for many years.

Public Perception and Critical Analysis Over Time

The public and critics alike have voiced their opinions over Agatha Christie's prolific works, starting with Christie's first published novel. In the beginning, Christie's reputation was that of a master storyteller, and she was regarded as an unparalleled achiever in "whodunit" novels. Several critiques have remarked, however, that her storytelling and characters were incredibly woven and bland and lacked creativity. This was the case until, with time, new angles of criticism opened, including understanding the relation of women and the working class and the more nuanced deeper context of her murder mysteries, which, alongside being simple, held more complex societal meanings.

Christie's work as an author was always accompanied by evolving public opinion and societal acceptance. Rethinking ethnography and Christie's portrayal of race in her work amplifies colonialism. Further developed studies and portrayals of women in her work and her role in the feminist movement brought massive attention. All the while, the number of readers interested in her works was unmatched, which attracted fundamental focus from literary historians.

The public perception of Christie's work has, like everything else, changed over the years. From being labelled as a writer of 'mere' popular fiction to being considered a prominent figure in the crime genre, Christie's work has always had an evolving outlook. The adaptation of her works into television shows and films has certainly changed how different generations perceive her writing. With every new adaptation or revival, the public always seems to revisit and rethink their relationship with her captivating stories, showcasing the dynamic nature of her legacy.

Without question, the critique and public perception of Agatha Christie's work are bound to change with changing literary fashions and evolving social values. Since her books are always in circulation and her works heavily influence contemporary crime fiction, the discussions around her work will always be highly contested.

Preservation of Christie's Original Works

Agatha Christie's works remain treasured for their complex plots, captivating characters, and unparalleled storytelling mastery. Moreover, her novels have significantly shaped the landscape of both crime fiction and classic literature. This impact should be remembered during discussions around the preservation of her original works. Christie's letters, manuscripts, and personal mementoes speak to her legacy; unlike other literary figures, her works occupy a dual position—they are treasured as mind-bending narratives and as cultural and historical artefacts. The urgency of preserving her works is paramount. Private collectors and academic institutions have come together to form The Agatha Christie Archive, which aids in preserving and celebrating the masterpieces through curatorial efforts. Her works demand attention beyond the physical manuscripts; there is an urgent need to digitise her corpus so future generations can access her literary artistry. Furthermore, active monitoring against unauthorised reproductions that compromise the integrity of Christie's works is essential. This includes safeguarding intellectual property rights and adhering to ethical standards concerning publications and adaptations of her works.

Christie's original works' preservation also covers fostering research, scholarship, and appreciation initiatives regarding her works' approaches. Christie's devotion has been exhibited by universities, libraries and literary societies that stage curated exhibitions or hold symposiums and provide research grants. These intellectual activities widen the scope of understanding storytelling strategies, Christie's thematics, and her instrumental sociocultural commentaries and critiques. Collaborations with preservation and archival science specialists guarantee the durability of her original manuscripts, and Christie's works are sheltered from the attack of time. Apart from the physical preservation, active steps are taken to inform and interest citizens on the subject of the greatest importance of her works. For instance, active means include outreach programmes, workshops and internet resources on the genesis and growth of her literary masterpieces. By promoting the appreciation of Christie's works, individuals and particular institutions sustain her literary legacies for the future. We take on a shared responsibility to ensure that her undisputed literary achievements will continue to be read for centuries.

By preserving her original pieces, we pay tribute to Agatha Christie's remarkable genius, mark her place within the literary edifice, and honour her everlasting impact on the world of mystery and thrill.

Final thoughts on an enduring legacy

While finalising our discussion around Agatha Christie's ever-evolving legacy, one observation stands out: She is perhaps the only author who cuts across centuries and geographical borders, marking different cultures. The overarching consistency of her artistry is such that every decade can extract something novel from her beautifully woven tales and the captivating characters within.

Her impact is not limited to spanning the boundaries of traditional crime fiction but reaches readers of different regions and cultures. Christie's unwavering reputation stems from her ability to weave together marvellous mysteries and insights into the human psyche. Her stories are timeless, reinforced by her status as a literary icon.

Last but not least, who can ignore Christie's impact on the development of the genre? The innovation she brought to her narrative structure, multifaceted storylines, and unforgettable characters like Poirot and Marple made her a precursor to modern crime fiction writers. Many contemporary authors consider her a key figure in developing their literature; Christie's impact has been profound and far-reaching.

Christie's legacy is in the academic world, where scholars analyse her works through a sociological, psychological, or literary lens. Her novels and short stories are replete with materials for academic critique, thereby enriching intellectual discourse and ensuring that her legacy endures in these hallowed halls.

Over the years, Christie's creations have had a substantial impact worldwide. Her books are bestsellers and await translation into a myriad of languages, allowing audiences from different regions to immerse in the brilliance of her storytelling. Translating her works into different cultures emphasises her universal appeal and cements her status as a literary figure who indelibly impacted the world.

Additionally, her works have been adapted into Christie's mysteries and brought to contemporary audiences through feature films and television series. These adaptations play a vital role in introducing her stories to younger generations, ensuring that her legacy is dynamic and alive in the present day.

The enduring influence of Christie's works has highlighted the recognition and accolades granted to her after she passed. Her contributions have received respect in the form of awards for crime fiction after her death, sustaining the legacy she left; this reinforces the Christine Award in 2011, which highlights the impact of her authors' success award Christie received in capped prison.

To conclude, Agatha Christie's legacy incorporates not only her literary works but also the literature, pop culture, and academic spheres covered by her books. Christie's ability to charm the attention of readers across all age groups, as well as the unfiltered enjoyment drawn from the reading, marks the dignity of Christie's literature and fortifies its aliment to the history of literature for centuries yet to follow.

Selected Bibliography

The Agatha Christie reading list

https://agathachristie.imgix.net/image-store/christie-reading-list.pdf

https://www.agathachristie.com/en

Miscellaneous sources and references

1. Biography of the Last Puffed Female Mystery Writer: Agatha Christie. (2023). *Pennsylvania Literary Journal, 15*(1), 49-52.

2. *Dining Room Detectives: Analysing Food in the Novels of Agatha Christie* (2015). . Cambridge Scholars Publisher Cambridge Scholars Publishing, Cambridge Scholars Publishing.

3. Murdering Memory and Sense. (2024). *Pennsylvania Literary Journal, 16*(3), 18-21,371.

4. The Life and Crimes of Agatha Christie: A Biographical Companion to the Works of Agatha Christie. (2000, 05). *Contemporary Review, 276*, 278.

5. Aldridge, M. (2016). *Agatha Christie on Screen*. Palgrave Macmillan Limited, Palgrave Macmillan Limited.

6. Ananya, D. G. (2023). Book Review of Kunal Basu's Filmi Stories: The Return of the Storyteller. *Contemporary Literary Review India, 10*(3), 197-207.

7. Atkins, I. K. (1975). Agatha Christie and the Detective Film: A Timetable for Success. *Literature/Film Quarterly, 3*(3), 205-214.

8. Bernthal, J. C. (2016). *Queering Agatha Christie: Revisiting the Golden Age of Detective Fiction*. Springer International Publishing AG, Springer International Publishing AG.

9. Beyer, C. (2023). "No Picturesque Village Is Safe":

Agatha Christie's Cornish Crime Scenes in "The Blood-Stained Pavement" and "Ingots of Gold". *Clues, 41*(1), 95-105.

10. Block, E. (2024). 'A LESS THAN PERFECT INSTRUMENT': BARBARA EHRENREICH'S STRUGGLE WITH THE INEFFABLE. *Renascence, 76*(2), 73-91,157.

11. Bloomfield, J. (2020). Mid-Century Jacobeans: Agatha Christie, Ngaio Marsh, P. D. James, and The Duchess of Malfi. *ELH, 87*(4), 1079-1104.

12. Botana, F. (2022). Tammaro De Marinis, Vittorio Forti, and the Acquisition of Islamic Manuscripts for J. P. Morgan in Constantinople in 1913. *Manuscript Studies, 7*(2), 237-269.

13. Brown, S. (2020). "Scoring Off a Foreigner?" Xenophobia, Antisemitism, and Racism in the Works of Agatha Christie. *Clues, 38*(1), 70-80.

14. Bubíková, Š., & Roebuck, O. (2024). Islands of Crime: The Island as a Setting in Crime Fiction. *Clues, 42*(1), 88-97.

15. Calhoun- French, D.,M. (2016). Agatha Christie's Secret Notebooks: Fifty Years of Mysteries in the Making/Agatha Christie: Murder in the Making-More Stories and Secrets from Her Notebooks.

Clues, 34(1), 152-154.

16. Corral, W. H. (2006). Doctor Pasavento. *World Literature Today, 80*(3), 71-72.

17. Cox, D. R. (2020). Charles Dickens's Last Case: Edwin Drood and the Curious Incident of the Unasked Question. *The Dickensian, 116*(511), 188.

18. Daniels, A. (2018). How Not To Be a Doctor and Other Essays. *The New Criterion, 37*(1), 65-67.

19. Daniels, A. (2020). Killing time with Agatha Christie. *The New Criterion, 39*(3), 34-37.

20. Davis, A. (2024). "A Modernist Lampstand": Noir and the Avant-garde in William Faulkner's Sanctuary. *Clues, 42*(1), 25-35.

21. Davis, J. M. (2014). Another Grand Master for Oklahoma. *World Literature Today, 88*(3), 9-11.

22. Davis, J. M. (2009). IF IT'S TUESDAY, THERE MUST BE A MURDER IN BELGIUM. *World Literature Today, 83*(4), 9-11.

23. Davis, J. M. (2016). Kiwi Crime Writing: A Rich Tradition from a Distant Sea. *World Literature Today, 90*(1), 16-18.

24. Davis, J. M. (2015). Playing by the Rules. *World Lit-*

erature Today, 89(3), 28-30.

25. Davis, J. M. (2023). The Enigma of Room 622. *World Literature Today, 97*(2), 80-81.

26. Davis, J. M. (2014). What She Laughingly Calls Her Career. *World Literature Today, 88*(1), 9-11.

27. Deutsch, A. R. P. (2024). Agatha Christie and the Guilty Pleasure of Poison. *Clues, 42*(1), 115-117.

28. DiGianvittorio, L., & Saunders, J. P. (2005). Janey Archer's Myopia and The Age of Innocence: [1]. *Edith Wharton Review, 21*(1), 15-18.

29. Eckert, K. (2021). Hercule Poirot and the Tricky Performers of Stereotypes in Agatha Christie's Murder on the Orient Express. *Text Matters,* (11), 186-203. https://doi.org/10.18778/2083-2931.11.13

30. Evans, M. A. (2023). Reading Crime Fiction, Writing Crime Fiction, and Overcoming the Tyranny of the Calendar. *Clues, 41*(2), 101-103.

31. Ewers, C. (2016). Genre in Transit: Agatha Christie, Trains, and the Whodunit. *Journal of Narrative Theory : JNT, 46*(1), 97-120,149.

32. Franks, R. (2016). Agatha Christie at Home. *Clues, 34*(1), 154-155.

33. Gillis, S. (2016). British Writers and the Approach of World War II. *Modernism/Modernity, 23*(2), 482-484.

34. Gillis, S. (2007). Detective Fiction. *Victorian Studies, 49*(2), 382-384.

35. Gretchko, J. M. J. (2024). Twenty-three Melville Letters That Have Appeared Since 1993: An Addendum to the Correspondence Volume. *Leviathan, 26*(1), 66-82. https://doi.org/10.1353/lvn.2024.a925511

36. Harmon, L. (2021). Agatha Christie's Poirot novels as fairy tales: Two case studies. *Literator, 42*(1)https://doi.org/10.4102/lit.v42i1.1756

37. Harrison, R. L. (2023). Eudora Welty and Mystery: Hidden in Plain Sight. *Legacy, 40*(1), 289-292.

38. Hassler, D. M. (2013). Generation and Energy. *Extrapolation., 54*(1), 112-114.

39. Henderson, H. (2024). Gender Roles and Political Contexts in Cold War Spy Fiction. *Clues, 42*(1), 112-114.

40. İlmek, S. T. (2020). Readers' voices for "complete retranslations": A case study of Agatha Christie's murder mysteries in Turkish. *Agathos, 11*(2), 161-175.

41. J, M. D. (2007). PORTRAIT OF AN ARTIST IN

A "SMALL" LANGUAGE. *World Literature Today, 81*(5), 6-7,5.

42. Jones, M. (2023). Introduction: Detective Fiction and Borders. *Clues, 41*(1), 5-12.

43. Karhulahti, V. (2015). An Ontological Theory of Narrative Works: Storygame as Postclassical Literature. *Storyworlds, 7*(1), 39-73,130.

44. Kaul, C. (2014). Book Review: India in Britain: South Asian Networks and Connections, 1858-1950. Susheila Nasta (ed.). Palgrave, 2013. *Literature & History, 23*(2), 98-100.

45. Kean, M. H. (2024). Beyond "Whodunnit". *The Baker Street Journal, Suppl.2024 Christmas Annual,* , 53-56.

46. Khalid, F. (2020). Good, Brave Causes: British Fiction of the 1950s. *Journal of Modern Literature, 44*(1), 191-196. https://doi.org/10.2979/jmodelite.44.1.13

47. King, S. (2018). E Pluribus Unum: A Transnational Reading of Agatha Christie's Murder on the Orient Express. *Clues, 36*(1), 9-19.

48. Kipen, D. (2013). Tinker Tailor Soldier Schreiber. *The Virginia Quarterly Review, 89*(1), 224-231,9.

49. Knepper, M. S. (2022). Agatha Christie and Hercule Poirot: The Greatest Mystery Writer and the Greatest Fictional Detective of All Time? *Clues, 40*(2), 127-130.

50. Knepper, M. S. (2008). Agatha Christie: Investigating Femininity. *Clues, 26*(3), 86-87.

51. Knepper, M. S. (2005). The Curtain Falls: Agatha Christie's Last Novels. *Clues, 23*(4), 69-84.

52. Köseoğlu, B. (2015). Gender and Detective Literature: The Role of Miss Marple in Agatha Christie's The Body in the Library. *International Journal of Applied Linguistics & English Literature, 4*(3), 132-137. https://doi.org/10.7575/aiac.ijalel.v.4n.3p.132

53. Krishnan, L. (2023, Spring). Brain or Appendix: Doctors, Detectives, and Diagnosis. *The Baker Street Journal, 73*, 7-17,76.

54. Laurence, J. (2016). Look to the Ladies. *World Literature Today, 90*(6), 22-24.

55. Majmudar, A. (2025). Scratched pads. *The New Criterion, 43*(6), 75-77.

56. Martin, S. (2018). Psychogeography and the Detective: Re- evaluating the Significance of Space in Agatha Christie's A Murder Is Announced. *Clues,*

36(1), 20-29.

57. Mezei, K. (2007). Spinsters, Surveillance, and Speech: The Case of Miss Marple, Miss Mole, and Miss Jekyll. *Journal of Modern Literature, 30*(2), 103-120.

58. Mills, R. (2019). "I Always Did Hate Watering-Places": Tourism and Carnival in Agatha Christie's and Dorothy L. Sayers's Seaside Novels. *Clues, 37*(2), 83-93.

59. Mirabile, M. (2010). British Literature of the Blitz: Fighting the People's War. *Modern Fiction Studies, 56*(3), 645-647.

60. Morris, M. A. (2010). "Canst thou draw out Leviathan with a hook?": Akunin Colludes and Collides with Collins and Christie. *Clues, 28*(1), 69-78.

61. Naidu, S. (2024). Interview with Kwei Quartey. *Clues, 42*(2), 138-143.

62. Naón, L. G. (2024, Mar). Recent Winners. *Poets & Writers, 52*, 89-97.

63. Northrup, T. (2015). Immoderate Families. *Canadian Literature*, (226), 156-157,170.

64. Oh, J. (2024). Grandma Detectives in Korea: Older Women Against the Crime of the "Silver Market". *Clues, 42*(2), 70-84.

65. Pamboukian, S. A. (2024). Witches and Pharmacists in Agatha Christie's The Pale Horse. *Clues, 42*(1), 75-87.

66. Panero, J. (2024). Brown in town. *The New Criterion, 42*(7), 52-55.

67. Percec, D., & Pungă, L. (2019). THEY DO IT WITH NURSERY RHYMES. THE MYSTERY OF INTERTEXTUALITY IN AGATHA CHRISTIE'S DETECTIVE FICTION FROM A LITERARY CRITIC'S AND A TRANSLATOR'S PERSPECTIVE. *British and American Studies, 25*, 247-256,282.

68. Perry, C. (2006). Book Review: Womens' Writing, 1945-1960: After the Deluge. Edited by Jane Dowson. Palgrave, 2003. *Literature & History, 15*(1), 89-91.

69. Query, P. (2008). Having Read Widely and Uncommonly Well. *Evelyn Waugh Newsletter and Studies, 38*(3), 1.

70. Reitz, C. (2024). Introduction: A Kaleidoscope of Cultures and Works. *Clues, 42*(1), 5-8.

71. Reitz, C. (2021). Introduction: So Many Books, So Little Time. *Clues, 39*(2), 5-7.

72. Riley, B. (2024). Under the Tuscan spell. *The New Criterion, 42*(8), 1-6.

73. Roger, P. (2013). Five French Critics. *New Literary History, 44*(2), 205-211,319.

74. Rolens, C. (2024). Latin American Detectives Against Power: Individualism, the State, and Failure in Crime Fiction. *Clues, 42*(1), 114-115.

75. Rowland, S. (2009). The Adventures of Margery Allingham. *Clues, 27*(2), 111-113.

76. Sandberg, E. (2019). "The Body in the Bath": Dorothy L. Sayers's Whose Body? and Embodied Detective Fiction. *Journal of Modern Literature, Suppl .Special Issue: Varieties of Embodiment: Whose Body?, 42*(2), 1-20. https://doi.org/10.2979/jmodelite.42.2.01

77. Schaffer, R. (2024). Animals in Detective Fiction. *Clues, 42*(2), 154-156.

78. Schaffer, R. (2023). Sleuthing Miss Marple: Gender, Genre, and Agency in Agatha Christie's Crime Fiction. *Clues, 41*(1), 140-142.

79. Simmons, L. K. (2015). The Artist and the Trinity: Dorothy L. Sayers' Theology of Work by Christine M. Fletcher (review). *Christianity & Literature, 64*(3),

334-337.

80. Sirvent, M. (1997). READER-INVESTIGATORS IN THE POST-NOUVEAU ROMAN: LAHOUGUE, PEETERS, AND PEREC. *Romanic Review, 88*(2), 315-335.

81. Smith, K. (2024). Rookies of the year. *The New Criterion, 43*(2), 1-8.

82. Sobanet, A. (2016). Mirror Gazing. *French Forum, 41*(3), 308-311.

83. Stewart, V. (2009). Spiritualism, Detective Fiction, and the Aftermath of War. *Clues, 27*(2), 75-84.

84. Strout, C. (2009). THE CASE OF THE MISSING NOVELIST: AMNESIA OR CONSPIRACY? *Sewanee Review, 117*(1), R15-R18.

85. Strout, C. (2007). THROUGH THE LOOKING GLASS AND BACK WITH AGATHA CHRISTIE. *Sewanee Review, 115*(1), 141-145,R24.

86. Teel, J. (2016). The Grand Tour: Around the World with the Queen of Mystery. *Clues, 34*(1), 157-158.

87. Valerie, W. W. (2023). Edgar and Me. *Poe Studies, 56*, 19-23.

88. Vanwesenbeeck, I. (2024). Icelandic Stories: A Con-

versation with Katrín Jakobsdóttir & Ragnar Jónasson. *World Literature Today, 98*(1), 19-23.

89. Vervel, M. (2022). "Mystery" Beyond Reason: Mr. Quin, A Revealer of the Powers of Fiction According to Agatha Christie? *Clues, 40*(2), 39-48.

90. Vujin, B., & Veselinović, S. (2024). Sleuthing from the Margins: Agatha Christie's Marple and Poirot as the Detecting Other. [Zasledovanje 7 obrobja: Marple in Poirot Agathe Christie kot zasledujoci Drugi] *Primerjalna Knjizevnost, 47*(3), 101-119.

91. Whitney, S. E. (2011). A Hidden Body in the Library: Mary Westmacott, Agatha Christie, and Emotional Violence. *Clues, 29*(1), 37-50.

92. Williams, R. (2011). Liminality in Fantastic Fiction: A Poststructuralist Approach. *Foundation, 40*(113), 84-89.

93. Yiannitsaros, C. (2017). "Tea and scandal at four-thirty": Fantasies of Englishness and Agatha Christie's Fiction of the 1930s and 1940s. *Clues, 35*(2), 78-88. Yiannitsaros, C. (2021). Delicious Death: Criminal Cake in and Beyond Agatha Christie's A Murder Is Announced. *Clues, 39*(2), 107-117.

94. Zsámba, R. (2017). Crime Fiction Reloaded. *HJEAS: Hungarian Journal of English and American Studies,*

23(1), 2254. Literature. (2021). *Old English Newsletter, 47*(1), 50-79.

95. *A Darker Shade of Sweden: Original Stories by Sweden's Greatest Crime Writers* (2014). . Grove/Atlantic, Incorporated, Grove/Atlantic, Incorporated.

96. *A Guide to Twentieth Century Literature in English* (2023). In Blamires H. (Ed.), . Taylor & Francis Group, Taylor & Francis Group.

97. *Andererseits - Yearbook of Transatlantic German Studies: Vol. 11/12, 2022/23* (2024). In Donahue W. C., Mein G. and Parr R.(Eds.), . transcript Verlag.

98. Aspects of Eve. (1975). *Aspects Of Eve, New York* ()

99. *Beyond Borders – Translations Moving Languages, Literatures and Cultures: Translations Moving Languages, Literatures and Cultures* (2011). In Kujamäki P., Kolehmainen L., Penttilä E. and Kemppanen H. (Eds.), . Frank & Timme, Frank & Timme.

100. Biographical Corner: Interview with Michael Bakewell by James Knowlson. (2023). *The Beckett Circle,* , 1-14.

101. Biography of the Last Puffed Female Mystery Writer: Agatha Christie. (2023). *Pennsylvania Literary Journal, 15*(1), 49-52.

102. *Comedy: American Style: Jessie Redmon Fauset* (2009). In Sherrard-Johnson C., Fauset J.(Eds.), . Rutgers University Press, Rutgers University Press.

103. *Crime Uncovered: Detective* (2015). In Forshaw B. (Ed.), . Intellect, Limited, Intellect, Limited.

104. *Dining Room Detectives: Analysing Food in the Novels of Agatha Christie* (2015). . Cambridge Scholars Publisher Cambridge Scholars Publishing, Cambridge Scholars Publishing.

105. *Fantastic Worlds: Myths, Tales, and Stories* (1996). In Rabkin E. S. (Ed.), . Oxford University Press, Incorporated, Oxford University Press, Incorporated.

106. Murdering Memory and Sense. (2024). *Pennsylvania Literary Journal, 16*(3), 18-21,371.

107. *Prison Writing: A Collection of Fact, Fiction and Verse* (2002). In Broadhead J., Kerr L.(Eds.), . Waterside Press, Waterside Press.

108. *Selected Letters of Katherine Anne Porter: Chronicles of a Modern Woman* (2012). In Unrue D. H. (Ed.), . University Press of Mississippi, University Press of Mississippi.

109. *Selected Letters of William Empson* (2006). In Haffenden J. (Ed.), . Oxford University Press, Incorpo-

rated, Oxford University Press, Incorporated.

110. *The Best American Essays 2017* (2017). In Jamison L. (Ed.), . Houghton Mifflin Harcourt Publishing Company, Houghton Mifflin Harcourt Publishing Company.

111. *The Best American Mystery Stories 2016* (2016). In George E. (Ed.), . Houghton Mifflin Harcourt Publishing Company, Houghton Mifflin Harcourt Publishing Company.

112. *The Letters of A. E. Housman: Two-Volume Set* (2007). In Burnett A. (Ed.), . Oxford University Press, Incorporated, Oxford University Press, Incorporated.

113. The Life and Crimes of Agatha Christie: A Biographical Companion to the Works of Agatha Christie. (2000, 05). *Contemporary Review, 276*, 278.

114. *The Shell Game: Writers Play with Borrowed Forms* (2018). In Adrian K. (Ed.), . University of Nebraska Press, University of Nebraska Press.

115. *Views from the Loft: A Portable Writer's Workshop* (2010). In Slager D. (Ed.), . Milkweed Editions, Milkweed Editions.

116. *Words We Call Home: Celebrating Creative Writing at UBC* (1990). In Svendsen L. (Ed.), . University of

British Columbia Press, University of British Columbia Press.

117. Aldridge, M. (2016). *Agatha Christie on Screen*. Palgrave Macmillan Limited, Palgrave Macmillan Limited.

118. Allen, B. (2013). Better than Brangelina. *The New Criterion, 31*(6), 1-4.

119. Ananya, D. G. (2023). Book Review of Kunal Basu's Filmi Stories: The Return of the Storyteller. *Contemporary Literary Review India, 10*(3), 197-207.

120. Andriacco, D. (2021, Autumn). Sherlock Holmes and the Development of the Detective Hero. *The Baker Street Journal, 71*, 22-28,68.

121. Anselmi, M. B. (2013). You Wouldn't Expect. *Obsidian., 14*(2), 37-64,95.

122. Arnautou, C. (2019). The Metaphysical Detective Fiction of G.K. Chesterton: "This is not a story of crime". *Études Anglaises, 72*(3), 291-308,378. Ashbery, J. (1995, 07). A poem of unrest / Tower of darkness / Theme / Sleepers Awake. *Poetry, 166*, 18

123. Ashbery, J. (1997). Sleepers Awake. *Can You Hear, Bird: Poems, New York* (pp. 99-100)

124. Atkins, I. K. (1975). Agatha Christie and the Detec-

tive Film: A Timetable for Success. *Literature/Film Quarterly, 3*(3), 205-214.

125. Bailey, J. T., & Strange, D. (2021). Notes. *The Thomas Wolfe Review, 44/45*(1), 182-240.

126. Banash, D. (2013). CRITIQUE: COLLAGE AND THE POLITICS OF THE CUT. *Postmodern Studies,* (49), 121-171,276-282.

127. Basu, R. (2005). *A Siren*

128. Bayer, D. (2021). *Tragödie des Rechts*. Duncker & Humblot.

129. Beeharry, D. C. (1979). *Three Women and a President.*

130. Bell, I. A., & Daldry, G. (1990). *Watching the detectives: essays on crime fiction*

131. Berensmeyer, I. (2016). "The musique concrète of civilization": Responding to Technological and Cultural Change in Postwar British Literature. *REAL, 32*(1), 169-186.

132. Berglund, L. (2012). "I AM LOST WITHOUT MY BOSWELL": SAMUEL JOHNSON AND SHERLOCK HOLMES. *The Age of Johnson, 22,* 131-XI.

133. Bernthal, J. C. (2016). *Queering Agatha Christie: Re-*

visiting the Golden Age of Detective Fiction. Springer International Publishing AG, Springer International Publishing AG.

134. Betz, P. M. (2018). Gender and Representation in British "Golden Age" Crime Fiction: Women Writing Women. *Clues, 36*(2), 120-122.

135. Beyer, C. (2023). "No Picturesque Village Is Safe": Agatha Christie's Cornish Crime Scenes in "The Blood-Stained Pavement" and "Ingots of Gold". *Clues, 41*(1), 95-105.

136. Birmelin, B. T. (2002). In her time. *Southwest Review, 87*(4), 511-527.

137. Bischoping, K., & Olstead, R. (2013). A "Beastly, Blood-Sucking Woman": Invocations of a Gothic Monster in Dorothy L. Sayers' Unnatural Death (1927). *The Irish Journal of Gothic and Horror Studies,* (12), 4-19,178.

138. Blasi, D. D. (2000). Czechoslovakian Rhapsody Sung to the Accompaniment of Piano. *Iowa Review, 30*(3), 29–45.

139. Block, E. (2024). 'A LESS THAN PERFECT INSTRUMENT': BARBARA EHRENREICH'S STRUGGLE WITH THE INEFFABLE. *Renascence, 76*(2), 73-91,157.

140. Bloomfield, J. (2020). Mid-Century Jacobeans: Agatha Christie, Ngaio Marsh, P. D. James, and The Duchess of Malfi. *ELH, 87*(4), 1079-1104. Blotner, J. (2005). *Faulkner: A Biography*. University Press of Mississippi, University Press of Mississippi.

141. Bond, R. (1993). *Once Upon a Mountain Time*. Penguin Books Ltd.

142. Bostrom, A. (2018). *Good Moaning France!: Officer Crabtree's Fronch Phrose Berk*. Waterside Press, Waterside Press.

143. Botana, F. (2022). Tammaro De Marinis, Vittorio Forti, and the Acquisition of Islamic Manuscripts for J. P. Morgan in Constantinople in 1913. *Manuscript Studies, 7*(2), 237-269.

144. Bouchardeau, H. (1998). *Agatha dans tous ses états*

145. Bouquet, P., & Voilley, P. (2000). *Droit et Littérature Dans le Contexte Suédois: Essai Sur la Littérature et le Droit*. Flies France SARL, Flies France SARL.

146. Bridgford, K. (1997). Snapshots. *The Massachusetts Review, 38*(2), 239-250.

147. Brown, S. (2020). "Scoring Off a Foreigner?" Xenophobia, Antisemitism, and Racism in the Works of Agatha Christie. *Clues, 38*(1), 70-80.

148. Brunsdale, M. M. (2010). *Icons of Mystery and Crime Detection: From Sleuths to Superheroes [2 Volumes].* Bloomsbury Publishing USA, Bloomsbury Publishing USA.

149. Bubíková, Š., & Roebuck, O. (2024). Islands of Crime: The Island as a Setting in Crime Fiction. *Clues, 42*(1), 88-97.

150. Calhoun- French, D.,M. (2016). Agatha Christie's Secret Notebooks: Fifty Years of Mysteries in the Making/Agatha Christie: Murder in the Making-More Stories and Secrets from Her Notebooks. *Clues, 34*(1), 152-154.

151. Cantu, N. E. (1995). *Canícula: Snapshots of a Girlhood en la Frontera*

152. Carter, D., & Osborne, R. (2018). *Australian Books and Authors in the American Marketplace 1840s–1940s.* Sydney University Press, Sydney University Press.

153. Cheung, E. M. K., & Leung, P. (2012). *City at the End of Time: Poems by Leung Ping-Kwan.* Hong Kong University Press, Hong Kong University Press.

154. Collyer, J. (1996, Spring). A businessman disappears. *The Paris Review, 38*, 242.

155. Condé, M. (2003). *Histoire de la Femme Cannibale*

156. Cook, M. (2014). *Detective Fiction and the Ghost Story: The Haunted Text*. Palgrave Macmillan Limited, Palgrave Macmillan Limited.

157. Corpi, L. (1992). *Eulogy for a Brown Angel*

158. Corral, W. H. (2006). Doctor Pasavento. *World Literature Today, 80*(3), 71-72.

159. Coward, N. (1999). *South Sea Bubble*

160. Cox, D. R. (2020). Charles Dickens's Last Case: Edwin Drood and the Curious Incident of the Unasked Question. *The Dickensian, 116*(511), 188. Cox, J. (2012). INTRODUCTION: BLURRING BOUNDARIES: THE FICTION OF M.E. BRADDON. *DQR Studies in Literature, 50*, 1-15,267-268.

161. Cox, R. (2018). The Mystery of Edwin Drood: Charles Dickens' Unfinished Novel and Our Endless Attempts to End It. *The Dickensian, 114*(506), 297.

162. Dalby, R. (1994). *The life and works of Agatha Christie*

163. Danebrock, F. (2023). *On Making Fiction: Frankenstein and the Life of Stories*. transcript Verlag, transcript Verlag.

164. Daniels, A. (2018). How Not To Be a Doctor and Other Essays. *The New Criterion, 37*(1), 65-67.

165. Daniels, A. (2020). Killing time with Agatha Christie. *The New Criterion, 39*(3), 34-37.

166. Davis, A. (2024). "A Modernist Lampstand": Noir and the Avant-garde in William Faulkner's Sanctuary. *Clues, 42*(1), 25-35.

167. Davis, J. M. (2014). Another Grand Master for Oklahoma. *World Literature Today, 88*(3), 9-11.

168. Davis, J. M. (2009). IF IT'S TUESDAY, THERE MUST BE A MURDER IN BELGIUM. *World Literature Today, 83*(4), 9-11.

169. Davis, J. M. (2016). Kiwi Crime Writing: A Rich Tradition from a Distant Sea. *World Literature Today, 90*(1), 16-18.

170. Davis, J. M. (2015). Playing by the Rules. *World Literature Today, 89*(3), 28-30. Davis, J. M. (2023). The Enigma of Room 622. *World Literature Today, 97*(2), 80-81.

171. Davis, J. M. (2014). What She Laughingly Calls Her Career. *World Literature Today, 88*(1), 9-11.

172. D'Cruze, S. (2006). 'The damned place was haunted': The Gothic, Middlebrow Culture and Inter-War

'Notable Trials'. *Literature & History, 15*(1), 37-58.

173. De Forest, J. W. (1867). *Miss Ravenel's Conversion from Secession to Loyalty*

174. De Forest, J. W. (1875). *Playing the Mischief: A Novel*

175. de Rooy, R. (2017). Divine Comics. *European Comic Art, 10*(1), 94-109. https://doi.org/10.3167/eca.2017.100108

176. DeCoste, D. M. (2013). "(AND YOU GET FAR TOO MUCH PUBLICITY ALREADY WHOEVER YOU ARE)"1: Gossip, Celebrity, and Modernist Authorship in Evelyn Waugh's Vile Bodies. *Papers on Language and Literature, 49*(1), 3-36.

177. Demastes, W. (2012). *The Cambridge Introduction to Tom Stoppard*. Cambridge University Press, Cambridge University Press.

178. Deutsch, A. R. P. (2024). Agatha Christie and the Guilty Pleasure of Poison. *Clues, 42*(1), 115-117.

179. DiGianvittorio, L., & Saunders, J. P. (2005). Janey Archer's Myopia and The Age of Innocence: [1]. *Edith Wharton Review, 21*(1), 15-18.

180. Dion, R., & Fortier, F. (2010). *Écrire l'écrivain: Formes contemporaines de la vie d'auteur*. Les Presses de l'Université de Montréal.

181. Doyle, A. C. (1993). In Green R. L. (Ed.), *Return of Sherlock Holmes*. Oxford University Press, Oxford University Press.

182. du Bearn, R. (1996, Summer). Clerihews for the Clerisy III. *The American Scholar, 65*, 356.

183. Duguid, L. (2007). *Anti-novelist?*

184. Durham, C. A. (2003). Modernism and mystery: The curious case of the Lost Generation. *Twentieth Century Literature, Suppl.Special Issue: American Writers and France, 49*(1), 82-102.

185. Eckert, K. (2021). Hercule Poirot and the Tricky Performers of Stereotypes in Agatha Christie's Murder on the Orient Express. *Text Matters,* (11), 186-203. https://doi.org/10.18778/2083-2931.11.13

186. Edmond, M. (2014). *Then It Was Now Again: Selected Critical Writing*. Atuanui Press, Atuanui Press.

187. Edwards, O. D. (2012). "THE HERO AS HISTORIAN": PIETER GEYL AND THE CONDITION OF CARLYLE AFTER HITLER. *Studies in the Literary Imagination, 45*(1), 167-185.

188. Erickson, R. (2023). Mabel Seeley's Intermodernist Crime Fiction. *The Space between, 19*, 1.

189. Evans, M. A. (2023). Reading Crime Fiction, Writing

Crime Fiction, and Overcoming the Tyranny of the Calendar. *Clues, 41*(2), 101-103.

190. Ewers, C. (2016). Genre in Transit: Agatha Christie, Trains, and the Whodunit. *Journal of Narrative Theory : JNT, 46*(1), 97-120,149.

191. Farmer, L. (2006). Christmas Eve. *Iowa Review, 35*(3), 130-136,178.

192. Farrington, A. (2008). Railway Killers. *Indiana Review, 30*(2), 5-21,148.

193. Fink, B. (2010). *The Psychoanalytic Adventures of Inspector Canal*. Karnac Books, Karnac Books.

194. Fowler, G. (2009). GAME'S END. *Sewanee Review, 117*(3), 378-393,R70.

195. Fox, K. (2019). *True Biographies of Nations: The Cultural Journeys of Dictionaries of National Biography*. ANU Press, ANU Press.

196. Franks, R. (2016). Agatha Christie at Home. *Clues, 34*(1), 154-155.

197. Freeman, C.,Jr. (2006). THE EDUCATION OF HENRY ADAMS. *Michigan Quarterly Review, 45*(3), 441-453,419.

198. Frelick, N. (2020). Gender, Transference, and the Re-

ception of Early Modern Women: The Case of Louise Labé. *Esprit Créateur, 60*(1), 9-22. https://doi.org/10.1353/esp.2020.0003

199. Geczy, A., & McBurnie, J. (2023). *Litcomix: Literary Theory and the Graphic Novel*. Rutgers University Press, Rutgers University Press.

200. Gillis, S. (2016). British Writers and the Approach of World War II. *Modernism/Modernity, 23*(2), 482-484.

201. Gillis, S. (2007). Detective Fiction. *Victorian Studies, 49*(2), 382-384.

202. Gilman, R. (2005). *The Drama Is Coming Now: The Theater Criticism of Richard Gilman, 1961-1991*. Yale University Press, Yale University Press.

203. Glenstone, S. (2005). THE STRUGGLES OF SHRIMP AND SQUIRREL. *The Massachusetts Review, 46*(2), 241-242,342.

204. Griffin, M. (2024). Of Gaines and Genre: Plotting the Racial Borders in Southern Louisiana. *The Mississippi Quarterly, 76*(2), 193-213. https://doi.org/10.1353/mss.2024.a928864

205. Gulddal, J., & Rolls, A. (2015). Mobile Criticism: Pierre Bayard's Irreverent Hermeneutics. *Australian*

Journal of French Studies, 52(1), 37-52. https://doi.org/10.3828/AJFS.2015.03

206. Harmon, L. (2021). Agatha Christie's Poirot novels as fairy tales: Two case studies. *Literator, 42*(1)https://doi.org/10.4102/lit.v42i1.1756

207. Harrison, R. L. (2023). Eudora Welty and Mystery: Hidden in Plain Sight. *Legacy, 40*(1), 289-292.

208. Hart, P. (1997). Historias de mujeres. *World Literature Today, 71*(4), 764-765.

209. Haskins, J. (2016). Fairweather Gods. *Iowa Review, 46*(1), 35-48,198-199.

210. Haslam, R. (2014). The Hermeneutic Hazards of Hibernicizing Oscar Wilde's The Picture of Dorian Gray. *English Literature in Transition, 1880-1920, 57*(1), 37-58.

211. Hassler, D. M. (2013). Generation and Energy. *Extrapolation., 54*(1), 112-114.

212. Hay, C. (2021). THE GUTHRIE REPORT AND ITS DISCONTENTS. *Australasian Drama Studies*, (78), 110-139,277.

213. Hellwig, H. (2023). *American Film Noir Genres, Characters, and Settings*. Lexington Books/Fortress Academic, Lexington Books/Fortress Academic.

214. Henderson, H. (2024). Gender Roles and Political Contexts in Cold War Spy Fiction. *Clues, 42*(1), 112-114.

215. Highway, T. (2015). *A Tale of Monstrous Extravagance: Imagining Multilingualism*. University of Alberta Press, University of Alberta Press.

216. Hinton, B., & Bell, J. (1989). *vii. Library Mystery*. Enitharmon Editions Limited.

217. Hoffman, M. (2016). *Gender and Representation in British 'Golden Age' Crime Fiction*. Palgrave Macmillan Limited, Palgrave Macmillan Limited.

218. Holly, G. J. (2005). Good Girl. *The Southern Review, 41*(3), 582-VII.

219. Holt, E. (2016). Amsterdam. *The Virginia Quarterly Review, 92*(4), 104-110,8.

220. İlmek, S. T. (2020). Readers' voices for "complete retranslations": A case study of Agatha Christie's murder mysteries in Turkish. *Agathos, 11*(2), 161-175.

221. Irimia, A. (2023). *Figures of Radical Absence: Blanks and Voids in Theory, Literature, and the Arts*. Walter de Gruyter GmbH, Walter de Gruyter GmbH.

222. Iroh, E. (1979). *Toads of War*. Heinemann.

223. J, M. D. (2007). PORTRAIT OF AN ARTIST IN A "SMALL" LANGUAGE. *World Literature Today, 81*(5), 6-7,5.

224. James Loe-Mie, F. (2002). *Voile de Misère sur les Filles de Cham: Roman*. Editions Orphie.

225. Johnson, G. M. (2008). Apparition of a Genre: The Psychical Case Study in the Pre-Modernist British Short Story. *Studies in the Fantastic,* (1), 3-17,126.

226. Jones, K. (2021). Almost Shakespeare – But Not Quite. *Critical Survey, 33*(2), 43-50. https://doi.org/10.3167/cs.2021.330205

227. Jones, M. (1994). "So many varieties of murder": Detection and biography in Coming through Slaughter. *Essays on Canadian Writing,* (53), 11-26.

228. Jones, M. (2023). Introduction: Detective Fiction and Borders. *Clues, 41*(1), 5-12.

229. Justice, J. R. (2009). THE SMELL OF ASHES. *Sewanee Review, 117*(3), 394-409,R70.

230. Kampa, S. (2011). *Cracks in the Invisible: Poems*. Ohio University Press, Ohio University Press.

231. Kanodia, A. (2023). Authorship and Adaptation: Study of the authors of Little Women. *Contemporary Literary Review India, 10*(1), 1-20.

232. Karhulahti, V. (2015). An Ontological Theory of Narrative Works: Storygame as Postclassical Literature. *Storyworlds, 7*(1), 39-73,130.

233. Kaul, C. (2014). Book Review: India in Britain: South Asian Networks and Connections, 1858-1950. Susheila Nasta (ed.). Palgrave, 2013. *Literature & History, 23*(2), 98-100.

234. Kawana, S. (2010). A Narrative Game of Cat and Mouse: Parody, Deception, and Fictional Whodunit in Natsume Soseki's Wagahai wa neko dearu. *Journal of Modern Literature, 33*(4), 1-20,199.

235. Kean, M. H. (2024). Beyond "Whodunnit". *The Baker Street Journal, Suppl.2024 Christmas Annual,* , 53-56.

236. Khalid, F. (2020). Good, Brave Causes: British Fiction of the 1950s. *Journal of Modern Literature, 44*(1), 191-196. https://doi.org/10.2979/jmodelite.44.1.13

237. Khedairi, B. (2009). Absent. *Southwest Review, 94*(1), 46-65,117.

238. Kiefer, J. (2008). Anatomy of a Janeite: Results from The Jane Austen Survey 2008. *Persuasions : The Jane Austen Journal on-Line, 29*(1)

239. King, S. (2018). E Pluribus Unum: A Transnational Reading of Agatha Christie's Murder on the Orient Express. *Clues, 36*(1), 9-19.

240. King, S. (2022). Rethinking Raymond Chandler's "The Simple Art of Murder" (1944/1946). *Clues, 40*(2), 9-17.

241. Kinsman, M. (2004). Introduction. *Clues, 23*(1), 4-7.

242. Kipen, D. (2013). Tinker Tailor Soldier Schreiber. *The Virginia Quarterly Review, 89*(1), 224-231,9.

243. Kitaiskaia, T. (2023). Engelond. *The Virginia Quarterly Review, 99*(3), 86.

244. Knepper, M. S. (2022). Agatha Christie and Hercule Poirot: The Greatest Mystery Writer and the Greatest Fictional Detective of All Time? *Clues, 40*(2), 127-130.

245. Knepper, M. S. (2008). Agatha Christie: Investigating Femininity. *Clues, 26*(3), 86-87.

246. Knepper, M. S. (2005). The Curtain Falls: Agatha Christie's Last Novels. *Clues, 23*(4), 69-84.

247. Köseoğlu, B. (2015). Gender and Detective Literature: The Role of Miss Marple in Agatha Christie's The Body in the Library. *International Journal of Applied Linguistics & English Literature, 4*(3), 132-137.

https://doi.org/10.7575/aiac.ijalel.v.4n.3p.132

248. Kraut, G. L. (2009). Simma Klepper Is Dead. *New England Review, 30*(2), 160-175,205.

249. Krishna, P. (2015). Efficient Breaches: A Romance. *The Virginia Quarterly Review, 91*(4), 126-135,8.

250. Krishnan, L. (2023, Spring). Brain or Appendix: Doctors, Detectives, and Diagnosis. *The Baker Street Journal, 73*, 7-17,76.

251. Lachman, M. (2019). *The Heirs of Anthony Boucher: A History of Mystery Fandom*. Sourcebooks, Incorporated, Sourcebooks, Incorporated.

252. Larson, K. A., & Paul, S. (2022). CURRENT BIBLIOGRAPHY. *The Hemingway Review, 42*(1), 118-130.

253. Laurence, J. (2016). Look to the Ladies. *World Literature Today, 90*(6), 22-24.

254. Levi, J. (2020). Ohaka Mairi. *Sewanee Review, 128*(3), 491-509. https://doi.org/10.1353/sew.2020.0035

255. Lyons, M. (2021). *The Typewriter Century: A Cultural History of Writing Practices*. University of Toronto Press, University of Toronto Press.

256. Martin, S. (2018). Psychogeography and the De-

tective: Re- evaluating the Significance of Space in Agatha Christie's A Murder Is Announced. *Clues, 36*(1), 20-29.

257. Mathur, M. (1990). General studies -- British Mystery Writers, 1920-1939 (Dictionary of Literary Biography, Volume 77) edited by Bernard Benstock and Thomas F. Staley. *Journal of Modern Literature, 17*(2-3), 192.

258. McAteer, C. (2020). *Translating Great Russian Literature: The Penguin Russian Classics*. Taylor & Francis Group, Taylor & Francis Group.

259. McCaffery, S. (2002). The Murder of Agatha Christie: a true story. *Seven Pages Missing: Volume II: Previously Uncollected Texts: 1968–2000, Toronto* (pp. 215-219)

260. McCaw, N. (2011). *Adapting Detective Fiction: Crime, Englishness and the TV Detectives*. Bloomsbury Publishing Plc, Bloomsbury Publishing Plc.

261. Mezei, K. (2007). Spinsters, Surveillance, and Speech: The Case of Miss Marple, Miss Mole, and Miss Jekyll. *Journal of Modern Literature, 30*(2), 103-120.

262. Mills, R. (2019). "I Always Did Hate Watering-Places": Tourism and Carnival in Agatha Christie's and Dorothy L. Sayers's Seaside Novels. *Clues, 37*(2),

83-93. Mirabile, M. (2010). British Literature of the Blitz: Fighting the People's War. *Modern Fiction Studies, 56*(3), 645-647.

263. Mizejewski, L. (2004). *Hardboiled and High Heeled: The Woman Detective in Popular Culture*. Taylor & Francis Group, Taylor & Francis Group.

264. Morgan, J. (1984). *Agatha Christie: a biography*.

265. Niemi, L. (2012). *The New Book of Plots: Constructing Engaging Narratives for Oral and Written Storytelling*. Parkhurst Brothers, Incorporated, Publishers, Parkhurst Brothers, Incorporated, Publishers.

266. Northrup, T. (2015). Immoderate Families. *Canadian Literature,* (226), 156-157,170.

267. Ofri, D. (2005). Maladies, Remedies, and Anthologies: Medicine Taken At Its Word. *Parnassus : Poetry in Review, 28*, 235-253,456.

268. Oh, J. (2024). Grandma Detectives in Korea: Older Women Against the Crime of the "Silver Market". *Clues, 42*(2), 70-84.

269. Omotoso, K. (1971). *The Edifice*. Heinemann.

270. O'Neill, H. (2018). *Wisdom in Nonsense: Invaluable Lessons from My Father*. University of Alberta Press, University of Alberta Press.

271. Pamboukian, S. (2017). Old Holmes: Sherlock, Testosterone, and "The Creeping Man". *Clues, 35*(1), 19-28.

272. Pamboukian, S. A. (2024). Witches and Pharmacists in Agatha Christie's The Pale Horse. *Clues, 42*(1), 75-87.

273. Pastan, L. (1975). AFTER AGATHA CHRISTIE. *Aspects Of Eve, New York* (pp. 43)

274. Pastan, L. (1982). After Agatha Christie. *Pm/Am: New and Selected Poems, New York* (pp. 54-55)

275. Pastan, L. (1998). After Agatha Christie. *Carnival Evening, London* (pp. 80-81)

276. Percec, D., & Pungă, L. (2019). THEY DO IT WITH NURSERY RHYMES. THE MYSTERY OF INTERTEXTUALITY IN AGATHA CHRISTIE'S DETECTIVE FICTION FROM A LITERARY CRITIC'S AND A TRANSLATOR'S PERSPECTIVE. *British and American Studies, 25*, 247-256,282.

277. Perry, C. (2006). Book Review: Womens' Writing, 1945-1960: After the Deluge. Edited by Jane Dowson. Palgrave, 2003. *Literature & History, 15*(1), 89-91.

278. Peters, A. (2005). A TRAVELER IN RESIDENCE: MAEVE BRENNAN AND THE LAST DAYS OF NEW YORK. *Women's Studies Quarterly, 33*(3), 66-89.

279. Petrie, G. (2000, Winter). Soldiers. *Confrontation, 70/71*, 190–203.

280. Plock, V. M. (2012). Sartorial Connections: Fashion, Clothes, and Character in Elizabeth Bowen's To the North. *Modernism/Modernity, 19*(2), 287-302.

281. Rolens, C. (2024). Latin American Detectives Against Power: Individualism, the State, and Failure in Crime Fiction. *Clues, 42*(1), 114-115.

282. Rousseau, M. C. (1981). SIR THOMAS MORE : UNE ÉNIGME RÉSOLUE ? *Moreana, 18*(71), 155-165.

283. Rowland, S. (2009). The Adventures of Margery Allingham. *Clues, 27*(2), 111-113.

284. S.J., P. B. E. (2010). Detective and Priest: The Paradoxes of Simenon's Maigret. *Christianity & Literature, 59*(3), 453-477.

285. Sandberg, E. (2019). "The Body in the Bath": Dorothy L. Sayers's Whose Body? and Embodied Detective Fiction. *Journal of Modern Literature, Suppl*

.Special Issue: Varieties of Embodiment: Whose Body?, *42*(2), 1-20. https://doi.org/10.2979/jmodelite.42.2.01

286. Sandwith, C. (2018). The Appearance of the Book: Towards a History of the Reading Lives and Worlds of Black South African Readers. *English in Africa, 45*(1), 11. https://doi.org/10.4314/eia.v45i1.1

287. Schaffer, R. (2024). Animals in Detective Fiction. *Clues, 42*(2), 154-156.

288. Schaffer, R. (2023). Sleuthing Miss Marple: Gender, Genre, and Agency in Agatha Christie's Crime Fiction. *Clues, 41*(1), 140-142.

289. Schall, J. V. (2000). *Schall on Chesterton: Timely Essays on Timeless Paradoxes*. Catholic University of America Press, Catholic University of America Press.

290. Schulte, E. (2010). A Space Between the Rows. *New England Review, 31*(1), 108-120,195.

291. Simmons, L. K. (2015). The Artist and the Trinity: Dorothy L. Sayers' Theology of Work by Christine M. Fletcher (review). *Christianity & Literature, 64*(3), 334-337.

292. Simon, N. (1991). *Biloxi Blues (The Brighton Beach Trilogy)*. Random House (UK).

293. Sirvent, M. (1997). READER-INVESTIGATORS IN THE POST-NOUVEAU ROMAN: LAHOUGUE, PEETERS, AND PEREC. *Romanic Review, 88*(2), 315-335.

294. Stewart, V. (2009). Spiritualism, Detective Fiction, and the Aftermath of War. *Clues, 27*(2), 75-84.

295. Strout, C. (2013). SHERLOCK EVERYWHERE. *Sewanee Review, 121*(3), 4-LI,LII,LIII,LXVII.

296. Strout, C. (2009). THE CASE OF THE MISSING NOVELIST: AMNESIA OR CONSPIRACY? *Sewanee Review, 117*(1), R15-R18.

297. Strout, C. (2007). THROUGH THE LOOKING GLASS AND BACK WITH AGATHA CHRISTIE. *Sewanee Review, 115*(1), 141-145,R24.

298. Suarez, V. (1995). *Havana Thursdays*

299. Subramanian, S. (2020). Jeeves Resumes Charge (A Contribution to the Literature on Reading Nietzsche). *Philosophy and Literature, 44*(2), 495-500.

300. Sutherland, J. (2012). *Lives of the Novelists: A History of Fiction in 294 Lives*. Yale University Press, Yale University Press.

301. Teel, J. (2016). The Grand Tour: Around the World with the Queen of Mystery. *Clues, 34*(1), 157-158.

302. Thompson, L. (2007). *Agatha Christie: an English mystery*. Headline.

303. Tusquets, E. (2014). Always the Sea. *New England Review, 35*(1), 133-134,198.

304. Updike, J. (1993). Agatha Christie and Beatrix Potter. *Collected Poems: 1953–1993, New York* (pp. 308-309)

305. Valerie, W. W. (2023). Edgar and Me. *Poe Studies, 56*, 19-23.

306. Vanwesenbeeck, I. (2024). Icelandic Stories: A Conversation with Katrín Jakobsdóttir & Ragnar Jónasson. *World Literature Today, 98*(1), 19-23.

307. Vervel, M. (2022). "Mystery" Beyond Reason: Mr. Quin, A Revealer of the Powers of Fiction According to Agatha Christie? *Clues, 40*(2), 39-48.

308. Vujin, B., & Veselinovié, S. (2024). Sleuthing from the Margins: Agatha Christie's Marple and Poirot as the Detecting Other. [Zasledovanje 7 obrobja: Marple in Poirot Agathe Christie kot zasledujoci Drugi] *Primerjalna Knjizevnost, 47*(3), 101-119.

309. W, R. G. (1998). Supralegal justice: Are real juries acting like fictional detectives? *Journal of American Culture, 21*(1), 1-5.

310. Wainwright, L. (2008). Solving Caribbean Mysteries:

Art, Embodiment and an Eye for the Tropics. *Small Axe, 12*(1), 133-144.

311. Warodell, J. A. (2016). The Writer at Work: Hand-Drawn Maps in Conrad's Manuscripts. *Conradiana, 48*(1), 25-45.

312. Webster, K. (2012). *Grand and Arsenal*. University of Iowa Press, University of Iowa Press.

313. Weissman, K. B. (2018). The Cliff. *Southwest Review, 103*(1), 76.

314. Wheeler, D. (2012). *Golden Age Drama in Contemporary Spain: The Comedia on Page, Stage and Screen*. Gwasg Prifysgol Cymru / University of Wales Press, Gwasg Prifysgol Cymru / University of Wales Press.

315. Whitney, S. E. (2011). A Hidden Body in the Library: Mary Westmacott, Agatha Christie, and Emotional Violence. *Clues, 29*(1), 37-50.

316. Wilkinson, E. (2009). A Murder Most Mysterious. *The Virginia Quarterly Review, 85*(1), 231-IX.

317. Williams, R. (2011). Liminality in Fantastic Fiction: A Poststructuralist Approach. *Foundation, 40*(113), 84-89.

318. Williams, T. (2007). Branch Lines. *The Dickensian, 103*(473), 269-272.

319. Witheford, H. (1994). *Fatality in the Canaries*. Faber & Faber.

320. Wood, M. (2024, Nov). Death of an Intelligence: Analog. *Analog Science Fiction & Fact, 144*, 78-87.

321. Woon, W. C. M. (2002). *The Advocate's Devil*

322. Yiannitsaros, C. (2017). "Tea and scandal at four-thirty": Fantasies of Englishness and Agatha Christie's Fiction of the 1930s and 1940s. *Clues, 35*(2), 78-88.

323. Yiannitsaros, C. (2021). Delicious Death: Criminal Cake in and Beyond Agatha Christie's A Murder Is Announced. *Clues, 39*(2), 107-117.

324. York, R. A. (2007). *Agatha Christie: Power and Illusion*. Palgrave Macmillan Limited, Palgrave Macmillan Limited.

325. Yup, P. (2015, Fall). Martine the West Nile Virus Specialist. *J Journal, 8*, 8-9,115.

326. Zsámba, R. (2017). Crime Fiction Reloaded. *HJEAS: Hungarian Journal of English and American Studies, 23*(1), 225-228,247.

www.ingramcontent.com/pod-product-compliance
Lightning Source LLC
Chambersburg PA
CBHW060355080526
44583CB00012B/323